501

MUST-TASTE COCKTAILS

501
MUST-TASTE COCKTAILS

Bounty Books

Publisher: Polly Manguel

Project Editor: Emma Beare

Publishing Assistant: Jo Archer

Contributing Editor: Cathy Lowne

Designer: Ron Callow/Design 23

Picture Researcher: Jennifer Veall

Production Manager: Neil Randles

First published in Great Britain in 2007 by Bounty Books,
a division of Octopus Publishing Group Limited

This edition published in 2007 by Bounty Books,
a division of Octopus Publishing Group Limited
2-4 Heron Quays, London E14 4JP

An Hachette Livre UK Company
Reprinted 2008

Copyright © 2007 Octopus Publishing Group Limited

A CIP catalogue record is available from the British Library

ISBN: 978-0-753716-43-4
Printed and bound in China

Notes

The measure that has been used in the recipes is based on a bar jigger, which is 1 oz. If
preferred, a different volume can be used, providing the proportions are kept constant within a
drink and suitable adjustments are made to spoon measurements, where they occur.

All recipes serve one unless otherwise specified.

Safety note

The Food and Drug Administration advises that eggs should not be consumed raw. This book
contains recipes made with raw eggs. It is prudent for more vulnerable people such as pregnant
and nursing mothers, invalids, and the elderly to avoid these recipes.

Contents

Introduction

Cocktails, whether served at a dedicated cocktail party or as a precursor to an elegant meal, lend an air of sophistication and glamor. There are hundreds and hundreds of different cocktails, some of which experience fleeting popularity before disappearing into obscurity while others remain popular for decades. In this book, the timeless favorites are collected together with more recent and modern classics.

But what exactly is a cocktail? Traditionally, they are mixed drinks, consisting of one or more liquors, together with flavorings such as fruit, fruit juice, liqueur, syrup, herbs, or spices. With a few exceptions, such as Flaming Lamborghini, they are chilled, shaken or stirred with ice, and served over ice or in chilled glasses. Long drinks, such as slings, are topped up with mixers, typically tonic water, soda water or cola. Many of them have traditional decorations—such as fruit wedges, swizzle sticks, green olives, or maraschino cherries—and are served in specific glasses. Good cocktails (except shots and slammers) are drinks to enjoy slowly. They look attractive, have a balance of flavors, and are appealing to both the eye and the palate

Why "cocktail"?

There are dozens of different possible sources for the word, including *coquetier*, a French egg-cup in which the drinks were served in a New Orleans bar in the early 19th century; a mixed-breed horse called a cock-tail; decocta, Latin for distilled; a cock's tail, either that worn by George Washington in his hat or by officers in a particular regiment, or one put into drinks to indicate that they contained alcohol; the tailings (dregs) at the bottom of a cask that were drained out through the cock (tap), mixed up, and sold cheaply; and "cock's ale", an ale served at cock fights and in which a sack of half-cooked chicken and other ingredients had been fermented for several days.

History

Flavoring liquors probably became popular because they were originally sold with a far higher alcohol content than they are now—up to 135° proof, instead of today's normal maximum of

Cosmopolitan
Cowgirl
Cranberry Crush
Crossbow
Cuba Libre
Cuban Breeze
Cucumber Sake-tini

Dark Knight
Decatini
Delft Donkey
Desert Daisy
Diamond Ring
Dirty Sanchez
Discovery Bay
Doobs Martini, The
Dragon's Fire

Early Night
East India
Eclipse
Egg Nog
El Diablo
El Dorado
Eve

Fair Lady
Fifth Avenue
Fighting Bob
Fireball
First the Money
Fish House Punch
Fix, The
Flaming Lamborghini
Florentine Coffee
Florida Skies
Flower Power Sour
Forest Fruit
Foxy's Millennium Punch
Fragrance
Franklin
French 75
French Kiss
French Leave

Frobisher
From the Rafters
Frostbite
Frosty Lime
Frozen Mango and Mint Spiced Daiquiri
Frozen Mango Daiquiri
Frozen Pineapple Daiquiri

Gauguin
Gimlet
Gin Cup
Gin Fizz
Gin Floradora
Gin Garden
Gin Sling
Gin and Tonic
Ginger Tom
Gingersnap
Glamour Martini, The
Go West
Godfather
Godfather Sour
Godmother
Golden Daisy
Golden Dawn
Gorgeous Grace
Grand Margarita
Grand Mimosa
Grandaddy Mimosa
Grapefruit Cooler
Grappa Manhattan
Grappa Strega
Grasshopper
Green Island Quiet Sunday
Grenada
Grenadine Soda

Hair Raiser
Haiti Punch
Harlequin (using apricot brandy)
Harlequin (using whisky)
Harvey Wallbanger
Havana Beach
Havana Zombie
Haven

Hawaiian Deluxe
Head-over-heels
Honey Water
Honeydew
Honeymoon
Hong Kong Sling
Honolulu
Hop Frog
Horse's Neck
Hummingbird
Hurricane

Iceberg
Iced Lemon and Mint Vodka
Illusion
Inspiration
Irish Coffee
Italian Heather

Jaffa
Jalisco Swizzle
Jersey Lily
Jolly Roger
Juliana Blue

Katinka
Keep Sober
Kinky Witch
Kir Champagne Royale
Kiss in the Dark
Kiwi Caipiroska
Kiwi in Tennessee, A
Knockout
Kurant Blush

La Seine Fizz
Lady of Leisure
Laila Cocktail
Le Mans
Legal High
Lemon Drop
Lemon Grass Collins

RUM

Gauguin

3 measures crushed ice
2 measures white rum
2 teaspoons passion fruit syrup
2 teaspoons lemon juice
1 teaspoon lime juice
maraschino cherry, to decorate

Put the crushed ice, rum, passion fruit syrup, and fruit juices into a food processor or blender and blend at a low speed for 15 seconds. Strain into a glass straight up and add a maraschino cherry to decorate.

Port Antonio

$\frac{1}{2}$ teaspoon grenadine
4–5 ice cubes
1 measure fresh lime juice
3 measures white or golden rum
lime zest, to decorate
maraschino cherry, to decorate

Spoon the grenadine into a chilled cocktail glass. Put the ice cubes into a mixing glass. Pour the lime juice and rum over the ice and stir vigorously, then strain into the cocktail glass. Wrap the lime zest around the cherry, impale them on a toothpick and use them to decorate the drink.

Port Antonio

Frozen Pineapple Daiquiri

crushed ice
2½ pineapple slices
½ measure fresh lime juice
1 measure white rum
¼ measure Cointreau
1 teaspoon sugar syrup
pineapple wedge, to decorate

Put some crushed ice into a food processor or blender. Add the pineapple
slices, lime juice, rum, Cointreau, and sugar syrup and blend until smooth.
Pour into a chilled Margarita glass and decorate with a pineapple wedge.

Frozen Mango and Mint Spiced Daiquiri

crushed ice
1 measure fresh lime juice
2 teaspoons sugar syrup
2 measures Captain Morgan Original Spiced Rum
$\frac{1}{2}$ ripe mango, peeled and roughly chopped
6 mint leaves
mango slice, to decorate
mint sprig, to decorate

Put some crushed ice in a food processor or blender. Add the lime juice, sugar syrup, rum, mango, and mint leaves and blend until smooth. Pour into a large Champagne saucer and decorate with a mango slice and a mint sprig.

Apricot Daiquiri

crushed ice
1 measure white rum
1 measure fresh lemon juice
1/2 measure apricot liqueur or brandy
3 ripe apricots, skinned and pitted
apricot slice, to decorate
maraschino cherry, to decorate
mint sprig, to decorate

Put some crushed ice into a food processor or blender. Add the rum, lemon juice, apricot liqueur or brandy and the prepared apricots and blend for 1 minute or until smooth. Pour into a chilled cocktail glass and decorate with an apricot slice, maraschino cherry and mint sprig.

Frozen Mango Daiquiri

crushed ice
1/2 mango, peeled and pitted
1 measure lime juice
2 measures white rum
1 teaspoon confectioner's sugar
mango slices, to decorate

Put a small scoop of crushed ice into a food processor or blender. Add the mango, lime juice, rum, and confectioner's sugar and blend until smooth. Serve in a large glass and decorate with mango slices.

Frozen Mango Daiquiri

Rum Old-fashioned

Rum Old-fashioned

3 ice cubes
1 dash Angostura bitters
1 dash lime bitters
1 teaspoon superfine sugar
1/2 measure water
2 measures white rum
1/2 measure dark rum
lime zest twist, to decorate

Stir 1 ice cube with the bitters, sugar, and water in a heavy-based old-fashioned glass until the sugar has dissolved. Add the white rum, stir, and add the remaining ice cubes. Add the dark rum and stir once again. Decorate with a lime zest twist.

El Dorado

4–5 ice cubes
1 measure white rum
1 measure advocaat
1 measure crème de cacao
2 teaspoons grated coconut

Put the ice cubes into a cocktail shaker. Pour the rum, advocaat, and crème de cacao over the ice and add the coconut. Shake until a frost forms, then strain into a chilled cocktail glass.

Black Widow

4–5 ice cubes
2 measures dark rum
1 measure Southern Comfort
juice of ½ lime
1 dash sugar syrup
lime slice, to decorate

Put the ice cubes into a cocktail shaker. Pour in the rum, Southern Comfort, lime juice, and sugar syrup and shake well. Strain into a chilled cocktail glass and decorate with a lime slice.

Mai Tai

ice cubes, and crushed ice
2 measures golden rum
½ measure orange Curaçao
½ measure orgeat syrup
juice of 1 lime
2 teaspoons Wood's Old Navy Rum
lime zest, to decorate
mint sprig, to decorate

Put some ice cubes with the golden rum, Curaçao, orgeat syrup, and lime juice into a cocktail shaker and shake well. Strain over crushed ice into an old-fashioned glass, float the Navy rum on top, and decorate with lime zest and a mint sprig.

Limon Mojito

1 lime, quartered
2 teaspoons light brown sugar
8 mint leaves
crushed ice
2 measures Bacardi Limón rum
soda water, to top up (optional)
lemon and lime slices, to decorate

Muddle the lime quarters, sugar, and mint in a highball glass. Fill the glass with crushed ice and add the rum. Stir and top up with soda water, if you like. Decorate with lemon and lime slices and serve with straws.

St Lucia

4–5 ice cubes
1 measure Curaçao
1 measure dry vermouth
juice of 1/2 orange
1 teaspoon grenadine
2 measures white or golden rum
orange zest spiral, to decorate
maraschino cherry, to decorate

Put the ice cubes into a cocktail shaker and pour them over the Curaçao, vermouth, orange juice, grenadine, and rum. Shake until a frost forms, then pour without straining into a highball glass. Decorate with an orange zest spiral and a maraschino cherry.

St Lucia

Coconut Daiquiri

4–5 crushed ice cubes
2 measures white rum
1 measure coconut liqueur
2 measures fresh lime juice
1 teaspoon grenadine
lime slice, to decorate

Put the crushed ice into a cocktail shaker. Pour the rum, coconut liqueur, lime juice, and grenadine over the ice and shake until a frost forms. Strain into a cocktail glass and decorate with a lime slice.

The Boadas Cocktail

1 measure white rum
1 measure red Dubonnet
1 measure orange Curaçao
maraschino cherries, to decorate

Stir the liquid in a mixing glass and pour into a small Martini glass. Decorate with maraschino cherries.

The Boadas Cocktail

Tobago

½ measure low-proof rum
½ measure gin
1 teaspoon lime juice
1 teaspoon guava syrup
crushed ice

Put the rum, gin, lime juice, and guava syrup into a cocktail shaker and shake well. Pour into a glass over crushed ice.

Florida Skies

cracked ice
1 measure white rum
¼ measure fresh lime juice
½ measure pineapple juice
soda water, to top up
cucumber or lime slices, to decorate

Put some cracked ice into a tall glass. Put the rum and fruit juices into a cocktail shaker. Shake lightly. Strain into the glass and top up with soda water. Decorate with cucumber or lime slices.

Florida Skies

Rum Crusta

lime wedge
superfine sugar
ice cubes, plus crushed ice to serve
2 measures dark rum
1 measure Cointreau
2 teaspoons Maraschino liqueur
2 teaspoons fresh lime juice
2 grapes, to decorate

Frost the rim of an old-fashioned glass by moistening it with the lime wedge and pressing it into the sugar. Put some ice cubes with the rum, Cointreau, Maraschino liqueur, and lime juice into a cocktail shaker and shake well. Strain into the old-fashioned glass filled with crushed ice and decorate with some grapes.

Havana Zombie

4–5 ice cubes
juice of 1 lime
5 tablespoons pineapple juice
1 teaspoon sugar syrup
1 measure white rum
1 measure golden rum
1 measure dark rum

Put the ice cubes into a mixing glass. Pour the fruit juices, sugar syrup, and rums over the ice and stir vigorously. Pour the cocktail, without straining, into a tall glass.

Hurricane

ice cubes
1 measure white rum
1 measure gold rum
2 teaspoons passion fruit syrup
2 teaspoons lime juice

Put some ice cubes into a cocktail shaker and pour over the rums, passion fruit syrup, and lime juice. Shake well. Strain the drink into a cocktail glass and add ice cubes.

Batiste

4–5 ice cubes
1 measure Grand Marnier
2 measures golden or dark rum

Put the ice cubes into a mixing glass. Pour the Grand Marnier and rum over the ice, stir vigorously, then strain into a cocktail glass.

Batiste

Pink Angel

ice cubes
1/2 measure white rum
1/4 measure advocaat
1/4 measure cherry brandy
1 egg white
1/2 measure heavy cream

Put some ice cubes with the rum, advocaat, cherry brandy, egg white, and cream into a cocktail shaker and shake well. Strain into a cocktail glass.

White Witch

8–10 ice cubes
1 measure white rum
1/2 measure white crème de cacao
1/2 measure Cointreau
juice of 1/2 lime
soda water, to top up
orange and lime slices, to decorate

Put half the ice cubes into a cocktail shaker and pour in the rum, crème de cacao, Cointreau, and lime juice. Shake and strain over the remaining ice cubes in an old-fashioned glass. Top up with soda water and stir to mix. Decorate with orange and lime slices and serve with straws.

White Witch

Mojito

Mojito

8 mint leaves
1/2 lime, cut into wedges
2 teaspoons cane sugar
crushed ice
2 1/2 measures white rum
soda water, to top up
mint sprigs, to decorate

Muddle the mint leaves, lime wedges, and sugar in a highball glass. Fill the glass with crushed ice and add the rum. Stir and top up with soda water. Decorate with mint sprigs.

Bolero

ice cubes
1 1/2 measures white rum
3/4 measure apple brandy
several drops sweet vermouth
lemon zest twist, to decorate

Put some ice into a cocktail shaker and pour the rum, apple brandy, and vermouth over it. Shake well. Strain into a glass and add ice cubes. Squeeze a lemon zest twist over the glass and drop it in.

Cooper Cooler

3–4 ice cubes
2 measures golden rum
3 measures dry ginger ale
1 tablespoon fresh lime or lemon juice
lime or lemon slice, to decorate

Put the ice cubes into a highball glass. Pour over the rum, dry ginger ale, and lime or lemon juice and stir. Decorate with lime or lemon slices.

Pink Mojito

6 mint leaves
1/2 lime
2 teaspoons sugar syrup
3 raspberries
crushed ice
1 1/2 measures white rum
1/2 measure Chambord raspberry liqueur
cranberry juice, to top up
mint sprig, to decorate

Muddle the mint leaves, lime, sugar syrup, and raspberries in a highball glass. Add some crushed ice and the rum and Chambord. Stir well and top up with cranberry juice. Decorate with a mint sprig.

Pink Mojito

Blue Hawaiian

crushed ice
1 measure white rum
$\frac{1}{2}$ measure blue Curaçao
2 measures pineapple juice
1 measure coconut cream
pineapple wedge, to decorate

Put some crushed ice into a food processor or blender and pour in the rum, Curaçao, pineapple juice, and coconut cream. Blend at high speed for 20–30 seconds. Pour into a chilled cocktail glass. Decorate with a pineapple wedge.

Pineapple Mojito

6 mint leaves
4 pineapple chunks
2 teaspoons light brown sugar
2 measures golden rum
crushed ice
pineapple juice, to top up
pineapple wedge, to decorate
mint sprig, to decorate

Muddle the mint leaves, pineapple chunks, and sugar in a cocktail shaker. Add the rum and shake well. Strain into a glass filled with crushed ice, top up with pineapple juice, and stir. Decorate with a pineapple wedge and a mint sprig.

Serenade

6 ice cubes, crushed
1 measure white rum
1/2 measure Amaretto di Saronno
1/2 measure coconut cream
2 measures pineapple juice
pineapple slice, to decorate

Put half the ice into a food processor or blender, add the rum, Amaretto di Saronno, coconut cream, and pineapple juice and blend for 20 seconds. Pour into a tall glass over the remaining ice cubes. Decorate with a pineapple slice and serve with a straw.

Discovery Bay

4–5 ice cubes
3 drops Angostura bitters
juice of 1/2 lime
1 teaspoon Curaçao or blue Curaçao
1 teaspoon sugar syrup
3 measures golden or dark rum
lime slices, to decorate

Put the ice cubes into a cocktail shaker, then shake the bitters over the ice. Pour in the lime juice, Curaçao, sugar syrup, and rum and shake until a frost forms. Strain into an old-fashioned glass. Decorate with lime slices.

Discovery Bay

Hawaiian Deluxe

Hawaiian Deluxe

ice cubes
1½ measures coconut rum
½ measure Cointreau
½ measure aged rum
1 measure coconut cream
2 measures pineapple juice
1 dash sugar syrup
1 dash lemon juice
1 dash grenadine
pineapple and coconut wedges, to decorate

Put some ice cubes with all the other ingredients, except the grenadine, into a cocktail shaker. Shake well. Strain into a large hurricane glass. Drizzle the grenadine on to the drink and decorate with pineapple and coconut wedges. Serve with long straws.

New Orleans Dandy

4–5 ice cubes
1 measure white rum
½ measure peach brandy
1 dash fresh orange juice
1 dash fresh lime juice
Champagne, to top up

Put the ice cubes into a cocktail shaker. Pour the rum, peach brandy, and fruit juices over the ice and shake until a frost forms. Strain into a Champagne flute or tall glass and top up with Champagne.

Cuba Libre

ice cubes
2 measures golden rum
juice of ½ lime
cola, to top up
lime wedges, to decorate

Fill a highball glass with ice cubes, pour over the rum and lime juice and stir to mix. Top up with cola and decorate with lime wedges.

I remember who first was cruel enough to nurture the cocktail party into life. But perhaps it would be not too much to say, in fact it would be not enough to say, that it was not worth the trouble. DOROTHY PARKER

Cuba Libre

First the Money (see page 59)

Banana Daiquiri

3 ice cubes, cracked
2 measures white rum
1/2 measure banana liqueur
1/2 small banana
1/2 measure lime cordial
1 teaspoon confectioner's sugar, to decorate
banana slice, to decorate

Put the cracked ice into a Margarita glass or tall goblet. Put the rum, banana liqueur, banana, and lime cordial into a food processor or blender and blend for 30 seconds. Pour into the glass and decorate with the confectioner's sugar and a banana slice.

Clem the Cuban

1 dash apple schnapps
1 mint sprig
2 lime wedges
1 measure Havana Club 3-year-old rum
crushed ice

Muddle the schnapps, mint sprig, and lime wedges in a cocktail shaker, then add the rum and a scoop of crushed ice. Shake very briefly and double strain into a shot glass.

Clem the Cuban

Red Rum

Red Rum

small handful of redcurrants
1/2 measure sloe gin
ice cubes
2 measures Bacardi 8-year-old rum
1/2 measure lemon juice
1/2 measure vanilla syrup
redcurrant string, to decorate

Muddle the redcurrants and sloe gin in a cocktail shaker. Add the ice cubes with the remaining ingredients and shake well. Double strain into a chilled Martini glass. Decorate with a redcurrant string.

Rude Jude

ice cubes
1 measure white rum
1 dash strawberry purée
1 dash strawberry syrup
1 dash fresh lime juice

Put some ice cubes into a cocktail shaker and pour the rum, strawberry purée, syrup, and lime juice over them. Shake well and strain into a shot glass.

Kinky Witch

ice cubes
1 measure Havana Club 3-year-old rum
1 measure Havana Club Silver Dry rum
1/2 measure orange Curaçao
1/2 measure crème de mure
1/2 measure orgeat syrup
2 measures orange juice
2 measures grapefruit juice
2 teaspoons overproof rum
grapefruit wedges, to decorate

Put some ice cubes with the Havana Club
rums, Curaçao, crème de mure, orgeat
syrup, and fruit juices into a cocktail shaker
and shake well. Strain into a highball glass
filled with ice cubes, float the overproof
rum over the surface, and decorate with
grapefruit wedges.

Work is the curse of the drinking class. OSCAR WILDE

Rum Refashioned

1 brown sugar cube
4 dashes Angostura bitters
ice cubes
2 measures aged rum
sugar syrup, to taste
lime zest twist, to decorate

Put the sugar cube into an old-fashioned glass, then splash in the bitters, add 2 ice cubes and stir. Add a quarter of the rum and another 2 ice cubes and stir. Continue building, and stirring, with the rum and ice cubes, adding sugar syrup to taste. Decorate with the lime zest twist.

Hummingbird

4–5 ice cubes, crushed
1 measure dark rum
1 measure light rum
1 measure Southern Comfort
1 measure fresh orange juice
cola, to top up
orange slice, to decorate

Put the crushed ice into a cocktail shaker. Pour the rums, Southern Comfort, and orange juice over the ice and shake until a frost forms. Strain into a long glass and top up with cola. Decorate with an orange slice and serve with a straw.

‘The important thing is the rhythm. Always have rhythm in your shaking. Now a Manhattan you always shake to fox-trot time, a Bronx to two-step time, a dry Martini you always shake to waltz time.’ WILLIAM POWELL, THE THIN MAN

Apple-soaked Mojito

8 mint leaves, plus a sprig to decorate
1/2 lime, cut into wedges
2 teaspoons sugar syrup
2 measures golden rum
crushed ice
1 measure apple juice
red apple slices, to decorate

Muddle the mint leaves, lime, and sugar syrup in a cocktail shaker. Add the rum and shake well. Strain into a highball glass filled with crushed ice and top up with apple juice. Decorate with a mint sprig and apple slices.

Tiki Treat

Tiki Treat

crushed ice
1/2 ripe mango, peeled and pitted, plus extra slices to decorate
3 coconut chunks
1 measure coconut cream
2 measures aged rum
dash lemon juice
1 teaspoon superfine sugar

Put a small scoop of crushed ice with all the other ingredients into a food processor or blender and blend until smooth. Serve in a stemmed hurricane glass with long straws and decorate with mango slices.

Jolly Roger

5 ice cubes, cracked
1 measure dark rum
1 measure Galliano
1/2 measure apricot brandy
3 measures orange juice
apricot, orange and lemon slices, to decorate

Put half of the cracked ice with the rum, Galliano, apricot brandy, and orange juice into a cocktail shaker and shake well. Strain over the remaining ice into a tall glass. Decorate with the fruit slices.

Strawberry and Mint Daiquiri

3 strawberries, hulled
1 dash strawberry syrup
6 mint leaves, plus extra sprig to decorate
ice cubes
2 measures golden rum
2 measures lime juice
strawberry slice, to decorate

Muddle the strawberries, strawberry syrup, and mint leaves in a cocktail shaker. Add some ice cubes with the rum and lime juice and shake well. Double strain into a chilled slim Martini glass. Decorate with a strawberry slice and a mint sprig.

Berlin Blonde

ice cubes
1 measure dark rum
1 measure Cointreau
1 measure heavy cream
ground cinnamon, to decorate
maraschino cherries, to decorate

Put some ice cubes with the rum, Cointreau, and cream into a cocktail shaker and shake well. Double strain into a chilled Martini glass. Decorate with a sprinkle of ground cinnamon and 2 maraschino cherries speared on a toothpick.

Chetta's Punch

ice cubes
2 measures Lamb's Navy Rum
2 measures undiluted blackcurrant cordial
1 tablespoon fresh lemon juice
6 dashes orange bitters
orange slices, to decorate

Put some ice cubes into a mixing glass with the rum, blackcurrant cordial, lemon juice, and bitters and stir well. Strain into an old-fashioned glass filled with ice cubes and decorate with orange slices.

Mafia Martini

ice cubes
2 measures golden rum
1/2 measure Chambord raspberry liqueur
1 measure apple juice
lime zest twist, to decorate

Put some ice cubes with the rum, Chambord, and apple juice into a cocktail shaker and shake briefly. Double strain into a chilled Martini glass. Decorate with a lime zest twist.

Mafia Martini

Cuban Breeze

ice cubes
3 measures cranberry juice
2 measures Havana Club 3-year-old rum
2 measures grapefruit juice
lime wedges, to decorate

Fill a highball glass with ice cubes and add the cranberry juice. Put some ice cubes into a cocktail shaker, add the rum and grapefruit juice, and shake to mix. Strain the mixture over the cranberry juice and decorate with lime wedges.

First the Money (see page 43)

1 lime
1 teaspoon white crème de menthe
crushed ice
1 measure dark rum
¾ measure Toussaint coffee liqueur
cola, to top up

Cut the lime into wedges and muddle with the crème de menthe in a highball glass. Fill the glass with crushed ice and add the rum and Toussaint. Top up with cola.

The really important things are said over cocktails and are never done. PETER F. DRUCKER

Almond Cigar

2 measures Havana Club 3-year-old rum
1 measure lime cordial
1 measure Amaretto di Saronno liqueur
cinnamon stick, to decorate
lime zest twist, to decorate

Pour the rum, lime cordial, and Amaretto di Saronno into a chilled cocktail
shaker. Shake and strain into a chilled Martini glass. Decorate with a
cinnamon stick and a lime zest twist.

Havana Beach

$\frac{1}{2}$ lime
2 measures pineapple juice
1 measure white rum
1 teaspoon sugar
dry ginger ale, to top up
lime slice, to decorate

Cut the lime into 4 pieces and put in a food processor or blender with the
pineapple juice, rum, and sugar. Blend until smooth. Pour into a hurricane
glass or large goblet and top up with dry ginger ale. Decorate with a lime
slice.

Havana Beach

My Tie Collection

ice cubes
2 measures golden rum
1 measure apple juice
1/2 measure fresh lime juice
1 dash orgeat syrup
6 mint leaves
2 teaspoons Wood's Old Navy Rum
maraschino cherry, to decorate
pineapple wedge, to decorate
lemon slice, to decorate

Put some ice cubes into a cocktail shaker with the golden rum, fruit juice, orgeat syrup, and mint leaves and shake well. Strain over ice cubes into a highball glass, float the Navy rum on top, and decorate with a cocktail cherry, a pineapple wedge, and a lemon slice.

Monoloco Zombie

ice cubes
1 measure white rum
1 measure Navy rum
1/2 measure apricot brandy
1/2 measure orange Curaçao
2 measures orange juice
2 measures pineapple juice
1/2 measure lime juice
1 dash grenadine
1/2 measure overproof rum
pineapple wedges, to decorate

Put some ice cubes with all the other ingredients, except the overproof rum, into a cocktail shaker. Shake well. Strain over some ice cubes in a large hurricane glass. Top with the overproof rum and decorate with pineapple wedges.

Pink Treasure

2 ice cubes, cracked
1 measure white rum
1 measure cherry brandy
bitter lemon or soda water, to taste (optional)
lemon zest spiral, to decorate

Put the cracked ice, rum, and cherry brandy into a glass. Add a splash of bitter lemon or soda water, if using. Decorate with a lemon zest spiral.

The Papa Doble

crushed ice
3 measures white rum
$1/2$ measure Maraschino liqueur
1 measure lime juice
$1^1/2$ measures grapefruit juice
grapefruit wedges, to decorate

Put a scoop of crushed ice with the rum, Maraschino liqueur, and fruit juices into a food processor or blender and blend until smooth. Serve in a highball glass with grapefruit wedges. This drink can be sweetened to taste with sugar syrup, although Hemingway never would.

The Papa Doble

Zombie

ice cubes
1 measure dark rum
1 measure white rum
1/2 measure golden rum
1/2 measure apricot brandy
juice of 1/2 lime
1 teaspoon grenadine
2 measures pineapple juice
1/2 measure sugar syrup
2 teaspoons overproof rum
pineapple wedge and leaf, to decorate
sugar, to decorate

Put some ice cubes into a cocktail shaker with the first 3 rums, apricot brandy, lime juice, grenadine, pineapple juice, and sugar syrup and shake well. Pour into a chilled glass without straining and float the overproof rum on top. Decorate with a pineapple wedge and leaf, and sprinkle a pinch of sugar over the top.

Grenada

4–5 ice cubes
juice of ½ orange
1 measure sweet vermouth
3 measures golden or dark rum
crumbled cinnamon stick, to decorate

Put the ice cubes in a mixing glass. Pour the orange juice, vermouth, and rum over the ice. Stir vigorously, then strain into a chilled cocktail glass. Sprinkle a little crumbled cinnamon stick on top.

Bahamas Punch

juice of 1 lemon
1 teaspoon sugar syrup
3 drops Angostura bitters
1/2 teaspoon grenadine
3 measures golden or white rum
orange and lemon slices
cracked ice
grated nutmeg, to decorate

Pour the lemon juice and sugar syrup into a mixing glass. Shake in the bitters, then add the grenadine, rum, and fruit. Stir and chill. To serve, fill an old-fashioned glass with cracked ice, pour in the punch without straining, and sprinkle with grated nutmeg.

Egg Nog

ice cubes
1 egg
1 tablespoon sugar syrup
2 measures rum
6 measures milk
grated nutmeg, to decorate

Half-fill a cocktail shaker with ice cubes. Add the egg, sugar syrup, rum, and milk and shake well for about 1 minute. Strain into a tumbler and sprinkle with a little grated nutmeg.

Egg Nog

Beautiful Beth

3–4 ice cubes, crushed
1 measure light rum
1 measure Malibu
1/2 measure Cointreau
chilled cola, to top up
maraschino cherries, to decorate

Put the ice cubes into a cocktail shaker. Pour the rum, Malibu, and Cointreau over the ice and shake until a frost forms. Strain into an old-fashioned glass and top up with chilled cola. Decorate with maraschino cherries impaled on a toothpick.

Passion for Fashion

ice cubes
1 1/2 measures golden rum
1/2 measure Grand Marnier
2 dashes Angostura bitters
pulp of 1 passion fruit
2 teaspoons passion fruit syrup
1 dash lime juice
maraschino cherries, to decorate

Put some ice cubes with the rum, Grand Marnier, bitters, passion fruit pulp and syrup, and lime juice into a cocktail shaker. Shake well. Double strain into a chilled Martini glass. Decorate with maraschino cherries.

Passion for Fashion

St Augustine

ice cubes
1½ measures white rum
1 measure grapefruit juice
1 teaspoon Cointreau
superfine sugar
lemon zest twist, to decorate

Put some ice cubes into a cocktail shaker and pour the rum, grapefruit juice, and Cointreau over them. Shake well. Frost the rim of a glass by dipping it into water, then pressing it into the sugar. Strain the drink into the prepared glass. Add ice cubes and a lemon zest twist.

Tropical Dream

3–4 ice cubes
1 measure white rum
1 measure Midori
1 tablespoon coconut cream
3 tablespoons pineapple juice
3 tablespoons fresh orange juice
½ measure crème de banane
½ banana
banana wedge with skin on, to decorate

Put the ice cubes into a food processor or blender with the rum, Midori, coconut cream, and fruit juices. Blend for about 10 seconds. Add the crème de banane and the banana and blend for a further 10 seconds. Pour into a tall glass, decorate with a banana wedge, and serve with a straw.

Tropical Dream

Piña Colada

ice cubes, cracked
1 measure white rum
2 measures coconut milk
2 measures pineapple juice
pineapple wedge, to decorate

Put some cracked ice, rum, coconut milk, and pineapple juice into a cocktail shaker. Shake lightly to mix. Strain into a large glass and decorate with the pineapple wedge.

Lobsters on South Beach

crushed ice
1 measure white rum
1 measure coconut rum
1 measure mango purée
2 measures mandarin juice (fresh if possible)
1 measure coconut cream
4 pineapple chunks
pineapple leaf, to decorate
mango slices, to decorate

Put some crushed ice with the rums, mango purée, mandarin juice, coconut cream, and pineapple chunks into a food processor or blender and blend until it is smooth. Serve in a large highball glass and decorate with a pineapple leaf and mango slices.

Piña Colada

Lobsters on South Beach

Yellow Bird

ice cubes
1½ measures rum
1 measure lime juice
½ measure Galliano
½ measure Triple Sec

Put the ice cubes into a cocktail shaker. Pour in the rum, lime juice, Galliano, and Triple Sec and shake well. Strain into a chilled cocktail glass.

Planter's Punch

ice cubes
2 measures Myer's Jamaican Planter's Punch rum
4 drops Angostura bitters
½ measure lime juice
2 measures chilled water
1 measure sugar syrup
orange and lime slices, to decorate

Put some ice cubes into a cocktail shaker with the rum, bitters, juice, water, and syrup. Shake well. Strain into a highball glass filled with ice cubes. Decorate with orange and lime slices.

Planter's Punch

Foxy's Millennium Punch

ice cubes
1½ measures white rum
1 measure dark rum
2 measures cranberry juice
2 measures guava juice
½ measure lime juice
pineapple and lime slices, to decorate
maraschino cherry, to decorate

Put some ice cubes into a large highball glass. Pour the rums and juices
over the ice and stir. Decorate with pineapple and lime slices and a
maraschino cherry, spiked on a toothpick.

Memorial services are the cocktail parties of the geriatric set.

HAROLD MACMILLAN

After Dark Crush

crushed ice
2 measures Barbadian rum
1/2 measure Koko Kanu (coconut rum)
1/2 measure vanilla syrup
1 measure coconut cream
soda water, to top up
maraschino cherries, to decorate

Fill a sling glass with crushed ice, then add, one by one, in order, the rums, vanilla syrup, and coconut cream. Stir and top up with soda water. Add more ice and decorate with maraschino cherries. Serve with long straws.

Bossanova

ice cubes
2 measures white rum
$\frac{1}{2}$ measure Galliano
$\frac{1}{2}$ measure apricot brandy
4 measures pressed apple juice
1 measure lime juice
$\frac{1}{2}$ measure sugar syrup
lime wedges, split, to decorate

Put some ice cubes with the rum, Galliano, apricot brandy, fruit juices, and syrup into a cocktail shaker and shake well. Strain into a highball glass filled with ice cubes. Decorate with split lime wedges and serve with long straws.

BRANDY

Toulon

4–5 ice cubes
1 measure dry vermouth
1 measure Bénédictine
3 measures brandy
orange zest strip, to decorate

Put the ice cubes into a mixing glass. Pour the vermouth, Bénédictine, and brandy over the ice and stir vigorously. Strain into a chilled cocktail glass and decorate with the orange zest strip.

American Rose

4–5 ice cubes, plus crushed ice to serve
1 measure brandy
1 dash Pernod
1 dash grenadine
1/2 ripe peach, skinned, pitted, and roughly chopped
Champagne, to top up
peach or mango slices, to decorate

Put the ice cubes into a cocktail shaker. Pour in the brandy, Pernod, and grenadine and add the peach. Shake well, then strain into a cocktail or Margarita glass filled with crushed ice. Top up with Champagne just before serving and add peach or mango slices to decorate.

American Rose

Shanghai

Shanghai

3 ice cubes, crushed
1 measure brandy
$\frac{1}{2}$ measure Curaçao
$\frac{1}{4}$ measure Maraschino liqueur
2 dashes Angostura bitters
lemon zest spiral, to decorate
maraschino cherry, to decorate

Put the crushed ice into a cocktail shaker. Add the brandy, Curaçao, Maraschino liqueur, and bitters and shake to mix. Pour into a cocktail glass and decorate with a lemon zest spiral and a maraschino cherry impaled on a toothpick.

Melbourne

4–5 ice cubes
1 measure Curaçao
3 measures brandy
lemon zest, to decorate

Put the ice cubes into a measuring glass, pour the Curaçao and brandy over them, and stir vigorously. Strain into a chilled cocktail glass. Squeeze the lemon zest over the drink, then drop it in.

Fifth Avenue

1 measure brown crème de cacao
1 measure apricot brandy
1 measure light cream

Pour the crème de cacao into a straight-sided liqueur glass. Using the back of a bar spoon, slowly float the apricot brandy over the crème de cacao. Pour the cream over the apricot brandy in the same way.

Corpse Reviver

3 ice cubes, cracked
2 measures brandy
1 measure Calvados
1 measure sweet vermouth
apple slice, to decorate

Put the cracked ice into a cocktail shaker. Add the brandy, Calvados, and vermouth and shake until a frost forms. Strain into a glass and decorate with an apple slice.

Penguin

1 measure brandy
1/2 measure Cointreau
1 measure fresh lemon juice
1 measure fresh orange juice
1 dash grenadine
ice cubes
1/4 orange slice, to decorate
1/4 lemon slice, to decorate

Pour the brandy, Cointreau, fruit juices, and grenadine into a mixing glass and stir well. Pour into a tall glass filled with ice cubes. Decorate with the orange and lemon slice quarters placed on the rim of the glass. Serve with 2 long straws.

Haiti Punch

2 pineapples, peeled and cubed
3 lemons, sliced
3 oranges, sliced
1 1/4 cups brandy
1 1/4 cups Orange Nassau liqueur
2 bottles sparkling dry white wine
pineapple leaf, to decorate
orange zest spiral, to decorate

Put the prepared fruit into a large bowl or pitcher and pour the brandy and Orange Nassau over it. Cover and chill for several hours. To serve, pour about 1 measure of the brandy mixture into a Champagne flute or tall glass, top up with sparkling wine, and add some of the pineapple cubes. Decorate with a pineapple leaf and orange zest spiral. Serves 12–15

Haiti Punch

Banana Bliss

4–5 ice cubes
1 measure brandy
1 measure crème de banane
1 measure Cointreau
lemon juice
banana wedge, to decorate

Put the ice cubes into a mixing glass and pour the brandy, crème de banane, and Cointreau over them. Stir with a spoon, then strain into a cocktail glass. Dip the banana wedge in lemon juice to prevent it discoloring and attach it to the rim of the glass.

One revolution is just like one cocktail, it just gets you organized for the next. WILL ROGERS

Spiced Sidecar

ice cubes
juice of ½ lemon
2 measures Captain Morgan Original Spiced Rum
1 measure brandy
1 measure Cointreau
lemon and orange zest twists, to decorate

Put some ice cubes into a cocktail shaker with the lemon juice, rum,
brandy, and Cointreau and shake well. Strain into an old-fashioned glass
filled with ice cubes and decorate with lemon and orange zest twists.

Brandied Boat

crushed ice
1 measure brandy
2 teaspoons lemon juice
1 teaspoon Maraschino bitters
1 measure port
lemon zest spiral, to decorate

Put the crushed ice into a cocktail shaker. Add the brandy, lemon juice, and bitters and shake to mix. Pour into a tumbler and then pour the port over the drink. Decorate with a lemon zest spiral on the side.

Big City Dog

2 dashes Peychaud's bitters
ice cubes
1 measure brandy
1/2 measure green Chartreuse
1/2 measure cherry brandy

Put the bitters into a brandy glass and swirl them around to coat the inside. Turn the glass upside down and let it drain. Put some ice cubes into a mixing glass with the brandy, green Chartreuse, and cherry brandy and stir well. Double strain into the brandy glass.

Angel Face

3 ice cubes, cracked
1 measure gin
1 measure apricot brandy
1 measure Calvados
orange zest twist, to decorate

Put the cracked ice into a cocktail shaker and pour the gin, apricot brandy, and Calvados over it. Shake well. Strain into a cocktail glass and add an orange zest twist.

Angel Face

Metropolitan

ice cubes, cracked
1 measure brandy
1 measure sweet vermouth
½ teaspoon sugar syrup
3–4 dashes Angostura bitters

Put some cracked ice into a cocktail shaker with the brandy, vermouth, sugar syrup, and bitters and shake well. Strain into a chilled cocktail glass.

Christmas Punch

juice of 15 lemons
juice of 4 oranges
2¹⁄₂ cups sugar
ice cubes
1¹⁄₄ cups orange Curaçao
2 measures grenadine
2 measures brandy
10 cups sparkling mineral water
orange and lemon zest, to decorate

Pour the fruit juices into a pitcher. Add the sugar and stir gently until it
has dissolved. Put a large quantity of ice cubes into a large punch bowl.
Add the fruit juices, Curaçao, grenadine, brandy, and mineral water and stir
well. Decorate with the orange and lemon zest before serving.
Serves 15–20

The trouble with jogging is that the ice falls out of your glass. MARTIN MULL

Brandy Crusta

lemon wedge
superfine sugar
ice cubes
2 measures brandy
½ measure orange Curaçao
½ measure Maraschino liqueur
1 measure fresh lemon juice
3 dashes Angostura bitters
lemon zest spiral, to decorate

Frost the rim of a chilled cocktail glass by moistening it with the lemon wedge then pressing it in the sugar. Put some ice cubes into a cocktail shaker with the brandy, Curaçao, Maraschino liqueur, lemon juice, and bitters and shake well. Strain into the prepared glass and decorate with lemon zest spiral.

Between the Sheets

4–5 ice cubes
1¼ measures brandy
1 measure white rum
½ measure Cointreau
¾ measure fresh lemon juice
½ measure sugar syrup

Put the ice cubes into a cocktail shaker. Add the brandy, rum, Cointreau, lemon juice, and sugar syrup and shake until a frost forms. Strain into a chilled cocktail glass.

Apple Posset

8 measures unsweetened apple juice
1 teaspoon light brown sugar
2 tablespoons Calvados
cinnamon stick

Heat the apple juice in a small saucepan to just below boiling point.
Meanwhile, measure the sugar and Calvados into a warmed mug or glass.
Pour the hot apple juice onto the sugar and Calvados, stirring with the
cinnamon stick until the sugar has dissolved.

Burnt Orange

4–5 ice cubes
3 drops orange bitters or Angostura bitters
juice of 1/2 orange
3 measures brandy
1/4 slice of orange, to decorate

Put the ice cubes into a cocktail shaker. Shake the bitters over the ice, add
the orange juice and brandy and shake vigorously. Strain into a chilled
cocktail glass and decorate with a quarter slice of orange.

Burnt Orange

Monta Rosa

4–5 ice cubes
juice of ½ lime
1 measure Cointreau
3 measures brandy

Put the ice cubes into a mixing glass. Pour the lime juice, Cointreau, and brandy over the ice and stir vigorously. Strain into a chilled cocktail glass.

Angel's Kiss

½ measure crème de cacao
½ measure brandy
½ measure lightly whipped heavy cream

Pour the crème de cacao into a shot glass. Using the back of a bar spoon, slowly float the brandy over the crème de cacao. Pour the cream over the brandy in the same way.

Caen-Caen

4–5 ice cubes
2 measures brandy
1 measure Calvados
1/2 measure sweet vermouth

Put the ice cubes into a mixing glass. Pour the brandy, Calvados, and vermouth over the ice and stir vigorously. Strain into a chilled cocktail glass.

Brandy Sidecar

4–5 ice cubes
juice of 1 lemon
1 measure Cointreau
2 measures brandy
orange zest spiral, to decorate
maraschino cherry, to decorate

Put the ice cubes into a mixing glass. Pour the lemon juice, Cointreau, and brandy over the ice and stir vigorously. Strain into a chilled cocktail glass. Decorate with an orange zest spiral and a cherry impaled on a toothpick.

East India

Hop Frog

ice cubes
1 measure brandy
2 measures lime juice

Put some ice cubes into a cocktail shaker with the other ingredients and shake well. Strain into a chilled cocktail glass.

East India

ice cubes
3 drops Angostura bitters
1/2 measure pineapple juice
1/2 measure blue Curaçao
2 measures brandy
orange zest spiral, to decorate

Put the ice cubes into a mixing glass. Shake the bitters over the ice and pour the pineapple juice, Curaçao, and brandy over it. Stir until frothy, then strain into a chilled cocktail glass. Decorate with an orange zest spiral tied into a knot.

Avondale Habit

3 strawberries, hulled
1 dash sugar syrup
4 mint leaves
crushed ice
1½ measures brandy
freshly cracked black pepper
2 teaspoons crème de menthe
mint sprig, to decorate
strawberry half, to decorate

Muddle the strawberries, sugar syrup, and mint leaves in an old-fashioned glass. Almost fill the glass with crushed ice, then add the brandy and cracked pepper. Stir and add more crushed ice, then add the crème de menthe. Decorate with a mint sprig and a strawberry half.

Stinger

4 ice cubes, cracked
½ measure white crème de menthe
1½ measures brandy
mint sprig, to decorate

Put the cracked ice into a cocktail shaker and pour the crème de menthe and brandy over it. Shake well. Strain into a cocktail or Margarita glass and decorate with a mint sprig.

Stinger

Avondale Habit

Leo

2–3 ice cubes, crushed
1 measure brandy
1½ measures fresh orange juice
½ measure Amaretto di Saronno liqueur
soda water, to taste
1 teaspoon Campari

Put the crushed ice into a cocktail shaker. Add the brandy, orange juice, and Amaretto di Saronno and shake well. Strain into a tall glass and add soda water, to taste, and the Campari.

Tidal Wave

6 ice cubes
1 measure Mandarine Napoléon brandy
4 measures bitter lemon
1 dash lemon juice
lemon slice, to decorate

Put the ice cubes into a highball glass. Add the Mandarine Napoléon, bitter lemon, and lemon juice and stir gently. Decorate with a lemon slice.

Tidal Wave

Parisien

Harlequin

lightly beaten egg white
superfine sugar
1 measure kirsch
1 measure apricot brandy
2 measures orange juice
soda water
orange slice, to decorate
2 maraschino cherries, to decorate

Frost the rim of a tumbler by dipping it into the egg white, then then pressing it into superfine sugar. Pour the kirsch, apricot brandy, and orange juice into a cocktail shaker. Shake lightly. Strain into the prepared glass and top up with soda water. Decorate with an orange slice and cherries.

Parisien

crushed ice
1 measure brandy
$\frac{1}{2}$ measure Calvados
1 measure fresh lemon juice
sugar syrup, to taste
$\frac{1}{2}$ measure Poire William liqueur
apple and pear slices, or seasonal fruits, to decorate

Fill a tumbler with crushed ice. Add the brandy, Calvados, lemon juice, and sugar syrup to taste. Pour the Poire William over the top and decorate with the fruit.

Apricot Sour

2 ice cubes, cracked
1 measure apricot brandy
1 measure lemon juice
1 dash Angostura bitters
1 dash egg white
1 apricot wedge, chopped
lemon slice, to decorate
maraschino cherry, to decorate

Put all the ingredients into a cocktail shaker and shake vigorously. Strain into a tumbler and decorate with a lemon slice and a maraschino cherry impaled on a toothpick.

Brandy Fix

1 teaspoon confectioner's sugar
1 teaspoon water
1 measure brandy
1/2 measure cherry brandy
juice of 1/2 lemon
crushed ice
lemon slice, to decorate

Dissolve the sugar in the water in a mixing glass, then add the brandy, cherry brandy, and lemon juice. Stir to mix. Pour into a brandy glass or small tumbler. Fill the glass with crushed ice, float a lemon slice on top, and serve with a straw.

Brandy Fix

Brandy Cuban

2–3 ice cubes
1$\frac{1}{2}$ measures brandy
juice of $\frac{1}{2}$ lime
cola, to top up
lime slice, to decorate

Put the ice cubes into a tumbler and pour the brandy and lime juice over them. Stir vigorously to mix. Top up with cola and decorate with a lime slice. Serve with a straw.

Monte Carlo Sling

5 seedless grapes, plus extra to decorate
crushed ice
1 measure brandy
$\frac{1}{2}$ measure peach liqueur
1 measure ruby port
1 measure lemon juice
$\frac{1}{2}$ measure orange juice
1 dash orange bitters
2 measures Champagne

Muddle the 5 grapes in a tall glass, then fill the glass with crushed ice. Put all the other ingredients, except the Champagne, into a cocktail shaker and add more ice. Shake well and strain into the glass. Top up with Champagne and decorate the glass with grapes.

Bedtime Bouncer

2 measures brandy
1 measure Cointreau
5 measures bitter lemon
4–6 ice cubes
lemon zest twist, to decorate

Pour the brandy, Cointreau, and bitter lemon into a tumbler, stir well and add the ice. Decorate with a lemon zest twist and serve with a straw.

Brandy Flip

ice cubes
1 egg
2 measures brandy
1½ teaspoons superfine sugar
grated nutmeg, to decorate

Put some ice cubes into a cocktail shaker with the egg, brandy, and sugar and shake well. Strain into a brandy glass and sprinkle a little grated nutmeg on top.

Brandy Classic

4–5 ice cubes, plus cracked ice to serve
1 measure brandy
1 measure blue Curaçao
1 measure Maraschino liqueur
juice of 1/2 lemon
lemon wedge, to decorate

Put the ice cubes into a cocktail shaker. Pour in the brandy, Curaçao, Maraschino liqueur, and lemon juice and shake to mix. Strain into a chilled cocktail glass. Add some cracked ice and a lemon wedge.

From the Rafters

ice cubes
1 measure brandy
1 tablespoon Frangelico hazelnut liqueur
1 measure Cointreau
1 measure pineapple juice
cherry slices, to decorate

Put some ice cubes into a cocktail shaker with the brandy, Frangelico liqueur, Cointreau, and pineapple juice and shake to mix. Strain into a chilled cocktail glass and decorate with cherry slices, which will sink to the bottom of the glass.

From the Rafters

American Beauty

4–5 ice cubes
1 measure brandy
1 measure dry vermouth
1 measure orange juice
1 measure grenadine
1 dash crème de menthe
2–3 dashes ruby port
maraschino cherry, to decorate
orange slice, to decorate
mint sprig, to decorate

Put the ice cubes into a cocktail shaker. Pour in the brandy, vermouth, orange juice, grenadine, and crème de menthe and shake well. Strain into a cocktail glass. Tilt the glass and gently pour in a little ruby port so that it floats on top. Decorate with a maraschino cherry, an orange slice, and a mint sprig impaled on a toothpick.

Morning

4–5 ice cubes
3 dashes Angostura bitters
5 dashes Pernod
1/2 teaspoon grenadine
1/2 teaspoon dry vermouth
1 measure Curaçao
3 measures brandy
maraschino cherries, to decorate

Put the ice cubes into a cocktail shaker. Shake the bitters over the ice and add the Pernod. Pour in the grenadine, vermouth, Curaçao, and brandy, shake well, then strain into a chilled cocktail or Margarita glass. Decorate with maraschino cherries impaled on a toothpick.

Morning

Sangria

Applejack Sour

ice cubes
2 measures apple brandy
½ measure lemon juice
1½ teaspoons sugar syrup

Put some ice cubes into a cocktail shaker and pour the apple brandy, lemon juice, and sugar syrup over them. Shake well. Strain into a sour glass and serve straight up or in an old-fashioned glass over ice.

Sangria

ice cubes
2 bottles light Spanish red wine, chilled
4 measures brandy
2 cups soda water, chilled
fruit in season, such as apples, pears, lemons, peaches, and strawberries, sliced
orange slices, to decorate

Put some ice cubes into a large bowl and pour the wine and brandy over them. Stir. Add the soda water and float the fruit on top. Serve in tall glasses and decorate with orange slices. Serves 10–12

Jaffa

3 ice cubes, cracked
1 measure Mandarine Napoléon brandy
1 measure brown crème de cacao
1 measure light cream
cocoa, to decorate

Put the cracked ice with the brandy, crème de cacao, and cream into a cocktail shaker and shake well. Strain into a chilled cocktail glass and sprinkle with cocoa.

Brandy Alexander

3 ice cubes, cracked
1 measure brandy
1 measure brown crème de cacao
1 measure light cream
cocoa, to decorate

Put the cracked ice with the brandy, crème de cacao and cream into a cocktail shaker and shake well. Strain into a chilled cocktail glass and sprinkle with cocoa.

Jaffa

Brandy Alexander

Fish House Punch

ice cubes
1 measure brandy
1 measure peach brandy
1 measure golden rum
1 measure lemon juice
1 measure cold English Breakfast tea
1/2 measure sugar syrup
soda water, to top up
lemon slice, to decorate

Put some ice cubes with the brandies, rum, lemon juice, tea, and sugar syrup into a cocktail shaker. Shake well. Double strain into a highball glass filled with ice cubes. Top up with soda water, decorate with a lemon slice, and serve with straws.

The Pudding Cocktail

1 measure Calvados
1½ measures brandy
1 egg yolk
1 teaspoon superfine sugar
ice cubes
ground cinnamon, to decorate

Put the Calvados, brandy, egg yolk, and superfine sugar into a shaker with some ice cubes and shake until well mixed. Strain into a chilled cocktail glass. Light a long taper, hold it over the glass, and sprinkle cinnamon through the flame on to the surface of the drink.

Nice Pear

ice cubes
2 measures brandy
1 measure Poire William liqueur
1 measure sweet vermouth
peeled pear slices, to decorate

Put some ice cubes into a cocktail shaker with the brandy, Poire William, and vermouth and shake well. Strain into a chilled cocktail glass and decorate with pear slices.

The cocktail party is a device for paying off obligations to people you don't want to invite for dinner. CHARLES SMITH

GIN

Sweet Sixteen

6–8 ice cubes
2 measures gin
juice of 1/2 lime
2 dashes grenadine
1 teaspoon sugar syrup
bitter lemon, to top up
lemon zest strip, to decorate

Put half of the ice cubes into a cocktail shaker and pour the gin, lime juice, grenadine, and sugar syrup over them. Shake until a frost forms. Put the remaining ice into a highball glass, strain the cocktail over the ice, and top up with bitter lemon. Decorate with a lemon zest strip.

Gimlet

2 measures gin
1 measure lime cordial
ice cubes
1/2 measure water
lime wedge, to decorate

Put the gin and lime cordial into a mixing glass, fill up with ice cubes, and stir well. Strain into a chilled cocktail glass, add the water, then squeeze the lime wedge into the cocktail before adding it to the drink.

Gimlet

Moon River

4–5 ice cubes
$\frac{1}{2}$ measure dry gin
$\frac{1}{2}$ measure apricot brandy
$\frac{1}{2}$ measure Cointreau
$\frac{1}{4}$ measure Galliano
$\frac{1}{4}$ measure fresh lemon juice
maraschino cherry, to decorate

Put some ice cubes into a mixing glass. Pour the gin, apricot brandy, Cointreau, Galliano, and lemon juice over the ice, stir, then strain into a large, chilled cocktail glass. Decorate with a maraschino cherry.

Luigi

ice cubes
1 measure fresh orange juice
1 measure dry vermouth
$\frac{1}{2}$ measure Cointreau
1 measure grenadine
2 measures gin
blood orange slice, to decorate

Put some ice cubes into a mixing glass. Pour the orange juice, vermouth, Cointreau, grenadine, and gin over the ice and stir vigorously. Strain into a chilled cocktail glass. Decorate with an orange slice.

Luigi

By Invitation Only

3 measures gin
2 teaspoons sugar syrup
2 teaspoons fresh lime juice
1 egg white
ice cubes
1 tablespoon crème de mure
blackberries, to decorate

Put the gin, sugar syrup, lime juice, and egg white into a cocktail shaker and shake to mix. Strain into a highball glass filled with ice cubes and lace with the crème de mure. Decorate with blackberries.

Honolulu

4–5 ice cubes
1 measure pineapple juice
1 measure fresh lemon juice
1 measure fresh orange juice
1/2 teaspoon grenadine
3 measures gin
pineapple slice, to decorate
maraschino cherry, to decorate

Put the ice cubes into a cocktail shaker and pour the fruit juices, grenadine, and gin over them. Shake until a frost forms. Strain into a chilled cocktail glass and decorate with a pineapple slice and a maraschino cherry.

Red Cloud

ice cubes
1½ measures gin
2 teaspoons apricot liqueur
2 teaspoons lemon juice
1 teaspoon grenadine
1–2 dashes Angostura bitters

Put some ice cubes into a cocktail shaker and pour the gin, apricot liqueur, lemon juice, grenadine, and bitters over them. Shake well, strain into a glass, and add more ice cubes.

New Orleans Dry Martini

5–6 ice cubes
2–3 drops Pernod
1 measure dry vermouth
4 measures gin

Put the ice cubes into a mixing glass. Pour the Pernod over the ice, then pour in the vermouth and gin. Stir (never shake) vigorously and evenly without splashing. Strain into a chilled cocktail glass.

**New Orleans
Dry Martini**

Negroni

Bitter-sweet Symphony

Bitter-sweet Symphony

ice cubes
1 measure gin
1 measure Campari
1/2 measure passion fruit syrup
1/2 measure fresh lemon juice
lemon slices, to decorate

Put some ice cubes into a cocktail shaker with the gin, Campari, passion fruit syrup, and lemon juice and shake to mix. Strain into an old-fashioned glass over 4–6 ice cubes and decorate with lemon slices.

Negroni

ice cubes
1 measure Plymouth gin
1 measure Campari
1 measure red vermouth
soda water, to top up (optional)
orange slices, to decorate

Put some ice cubes into a cocktail shaker with the gin, Campari, and vermouth and shake to mix. Strain into an old-fashioned glass filled with ice cubes, top up with soda water, if you like, and decorate with orange slices.

Delft Donkey

3–4 ice cubes, cracked
2 measures gin
juice of 1 lemon
ginger beer, to top up
lemon slice, to decorate

Put the cracked ice into a cocktail shaker and pour the gin and lemon juice over it. Shake until a frost forms. Pour into a hurricane glass or large tumbler and top up with ginger beer. Decorate with a lemon slice and serve with a straw.

Sapphire Martini

4 ice cubes
2 measures gin
1/2 measure blue Curaçao
red or blue maraschino cherry, to decorate

Put the ice cubes into a cocktail shaker. Pour in the gin and blue Curaçao. Shake well to mix. Strain into a cocktail glass and carefully drop in a blue or red maraschino cherry.

Sapphire Martini

Zaza

5–6 ice cubes
3 drops orange bitters
1 measure Dubonnet
2 measures gin

Put the ice cubes into a mixing glass. Shake the bitters over the ice, pour in the Dubonnet, and gin and stir vigorously without splashing. Strain into a chilled cocktail glass.

Pink Clover Club

4–5 ice cubes
juice of 1 lime
1 dash grenadine
1 egg white
3 measures gin
strawberry slice, to decorate

Put the ice cubes into a cocktail shaker. Pour the lime juice, grenadine, egg white, and gin over the ice. Shake until a frost forms, then strain into a cocktail glass. Decorate with a strawberry slice and serve with a straw.

Pink Clover Club

Turf

ice cubes
1 measure gin
1 measure dry vermouth
1 teaspoon lemon juice
1 teaspoon Pernod
lemon slice, to decorate

Put some ice cubes into a cocktail shaker and pour the gin, vermouth, lemon juice, and Pernod over them. Shake well, then strain into a glass containing more ice. Decorate with a lemon slice.

Gin Cup

3 mint sprigs, plus extra to decorate
1 teaspoon sugar syrup
ice cubes, cracked
juice of ½ lemon
3 measures gin

Muddle the mint and sugar syrup in an old-fashioned glass. Fill the glass with cracked ice, add the lemon juice and gin, and stir until a frost begins to form. Decorate with extra mint sprigs.

Gin Cup

Ruby Fizz

ice cubes
juice of 1/2 lemon
1 teaspoon granulated sugar
1 egg white
2 measures sloe gin
2 dashes raspberry syrup or grenadine
soda water, to top up

Put some ice cubes into a cocktail shaker. Add the lemon juice, sugar, egg white, gin, and raspberry syrup or grenadine. Shake well, strain into a tall tumbler, and top up with the soda water.

Mbolero

2 lime wedges
2 measures gin
6 mint leaves, plus extra sprig to decorate
6 drops orange bitters
1 dash sugar syrup
ice cubes

Squeeze the lime wedges into a cocktail shaker. Add the gin, mint leaves, bitters, sugar syrup, and some ice cubes and shake well. Double strain into a chilled Martini glass. Decorate with a mint sprig.

Mbolero

Paradise

Paradise

3 ice cubes, cracked
1 dash fresh lemon juice
1/2 measure fresh orange juice
1 measure gin
1/2 measure apricot brandy
orange and lemon slices, to decorate

Put the cracked ice into a cocktail shaker. Pour the fruit juices, gin, and apricot brandy over it and and shake well. Strain into a chilled cocktail glass and decorate with orange and lemon slices.

Monkey Gland

3–4 ice cubes
1 measure orange juice
2 measures gin
3 dashes Pernod
3 dashes grenadine

Put the ice cubes into a cocktail shaker with the orange juice, gin, Pernod, and grenadine. Shake well, then strain into a chilled cocktail glass.

Stormy Weather

3 ice cubes, cracked
1$\frac{1}{2}$ measures gin
$\frac{1}{4}$ Mandarine Napoléon brandy
$\frac{1}{4}$ measure dry vermouth
$\frac{1}{4}$ measure sweet vermouth
orange zest spiral, to decorate

Put the cracked ice into a cocktail shaker and add the gin, Mandarine Napoléon, and the vermouths. Shake to mix and strain into a chilled cocktail glass. Decorate the rim of the glass with an orange zest spiral.

Bijou

3 ice cubes
1 measure gin
$\frac{1}{2}$ measure green Chartreuse
$\frac{1}{2}$ measure sweet vermouth
1 dash orange bitters
green olives, to decorate
lemon zest, to decorate

Put the ice cubes into a mixing glass and add the gin, Chartreuse, vermouth, and bitters. Stir well and strain into a cocktail glass. Impale the olives on a toothpick and add to the cocktail, then squeeze the lemon zest over the surface and drop it in.

Park Lane Special

ice cubes
2 measures gin
1/2 measure apricot brandy
1/2 measure fresh orange juice
1 dash grenadine
1/2 egg white

Put some ice cubes into a cocktail shaker and pour the remaining ingredients over them. Shake well and strain into a cocktail glass.

Smoky

ice cubes
1/4 measure dry vermouth
2 measures gin
1 measure sloe gin
5 drops of orange bitters
orange zest twist, to decorate

Put the ice cubes into a mixing glass, add the vermouth, and stir until the ice cubes are well coated. Pour in the gin, sloe gin, and bitters and stir well, then strain into a chilled cocktail glass and add an orange zest twist.

Broadhurst Drive-by

ice cubes
1½ measures gin
1 measure sweet vermouth
1 dash fresh lime juice
1 measure apple juice
green apple slice, to decorate
maraschino cherry, to decorate

Put some ice cubes with the gin, vermouth, and fruit juices into a cocktail shaker and shake to mix. Strain into an old-fashioned glass and decorate with a green apple slice and a maraschino cherry impaled on a toothpick.

Bronx

cracked ice, plus ice cubes to serve
1 measure gin
1 measure sweet vermouth
1 measure dry vermouth
2 measures orange juice
orange slices, to decorate
maraschino cherry, to decorate (optional)

Put some cracked ice into a cocktail shaker and pour the gin, vermouths, and orange juice over it. Shake to mix. Strain into an old-fashioned glass over some ice cubes. Decorate with orange slices and a maraschino cherry, if you like.

Broadhurst Drive-by

Bronx

Ginger Tom

Ginger Tom

ice cubes
1½ measures gin
1 measure Cointreau
1 dash fresh lime juice
1 dash sweetened ginger syrup
1½ measures cranberry juice
lime zest spiral, to decorate

Put some ice cubes into a cocktail shaker with the gin, Cointreau, lime juice, ginger syrup, and cranberry juice and shake to mix. Strain into a chilled cocktail glass and decorate with a lime zest spiral.

Pink Gin

1–4 dashes Angostura bitters
1 measure gin
iced water, to top up

Shake the bitters into a cocktail glass and swirl them around to coat the inside. Add the gin, then top up with iced water to taste.

Horse's Neck

4–6 ice cubes
1½ measures gin
dry ginger ale, to top up
lemon zest spiral, to decorate

Put the ice cubes into a tall glass and pour in the gin. Top up with ginger ale, then dangle the lemon zest spiral over the edge of the glass.

Opera

4–5 ice cubes
1 measure Dubonnet
½ measure Curaçao
2 measures gin
orange zest spiral, to decorate

Put the ice cubes into a mixing glass. Pour the Dubonnet, Curaçao, and gin over the ice. Stir evenly, then strain into a chilled cocktail glass. Decorate with an orange zest spiral.

Opera

Sydney Fizz

4–5 ice cubes
1 measure fresh lemon juice
1 measure fresh orange juice
1/2 teaspoon grenadine
3 measures gin
soda water, to top up
orange slice, to decorate

Put the ice cubes into a cocktail shaker. Pour the fruit juices, grenadine, and gin over the ice and shake vigorously until a frost forms. Strain into an old-fashioned glass and top up with soda water. Decorate with the orange slice.

Franklin

1/2 measure dry vermouth
3 measures ice-cold gin
2 green olives or lemon zest twist, to decorate

Swirl the vermouth around the inside of a chilled Martini glass, then discard the excess. Pour in the ice-cold gin and add the olives or lemon zest twist.

Franklin

San Francisco

ice cubes
1½ measures sloe gin
¼ measure sweet vermouth
¼ measure dry vermouth
1 dash orange bitters
1 dash Angostura bitters
maraschino cherry, to decorate

Put some ice cubes into a mixing glass. Add the gin, vermouths, and bitters and stir well. Pour into a cocktail glass and decorate with a maraschino cherry.

Of all the gin joints in all the towns in all the world, she walks into mine.

RICK BLAINE, CASABLANCA

Collinson

3 ice cubes, cracked
1 dash orange bitters
1 measure gin
1/2 measure dry vermouth
1/4 measure kirsch
lemon zest
1/2 strawberry, to decorate
1 lemon slice, to decorate

Put the cracked ice into a mixing glass, then add the bitters, gin, vermouth, and kirsch. Stir well and strain into a cocktail glass. Squeeze the lemon zest over the surface and decorate the rim of the glass with the strawberry half and lemon slice.

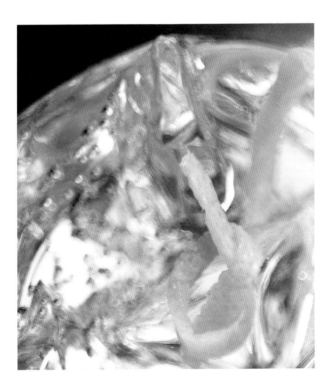

White Lady

Lady of Leisure

White Lady

1 measure gin
1 measure Cointreau
1 measure lemon juice
lemon zest twist, to decorate (optional)

Pour the gin, Cointreau and lemon juice into a cocktail shaker. Shake well, strain into a chilled Martini glass, and decorate with a lemon zest twist if you like.

Lady of Leisure

ice cubes
1 measure gin
1/2 measure Chambord raspberry liqueur
1/2 measure Cointreau
1 dash fresh lemon juice
1 measure pineapple juice
orange zest strips, to decorate

Put some ice cubes into a cocktail shaker with the gin, Chambord, Cointreau, and fruit juices and shake to mix. Strain into a chilled cocktail glass and decorate with orange zest strips.

Gin and Tonic

ice cubes
2 measures gin
4 measures tonic water
2 lime wedges, to decorate

Fill a highball glass with ice cubes, pour in the gin and then the tonic water. Decorate with lime wedges.

Tanqstream

ice cubes, cracked
2 measures Tanqueray gin
2 teaspoons fresh lime juice
3 measures soda water or tonic water
2 teaspoons crème de cassis
lime slices, to decorate
fresh blackcurrants or blueberries, to decorate (optional)

Put some cracked ice into a cocktail shaker and shake to mix with the gin and lime juice. Strain into a highball glass half-filled with cracked ice. For a dry Tanqstream, add soda water; for a less dry drink, add tonic water. Stir in the cassis and decorate with the lime slices and fresh fruit, if you like.

Gin and Tonic

Tanqstream

Albemarle Fizz

4–6 ice cubes
1 measure Tanqueray gin
juice of 1/2 lemon
2 dashes raspberry syrup
1/2 teaspoon sugar syrup
soda water, to top up
maraschino cherries, to decorate

Put half of the ice cubes into a mixing glass and add the gin, lemon juice, and raspberry and sugar syrups. Stir to mix, then strain into a highball glass. Add the remaining ice cubes and top up with soda water. Decorate with two maraschino cherries impaled on a toothpick and serve with straws.

Aviation

ice cubes
2 measures gin
1/2 measure Maraschino liqueur
1/2 measure lemon juice
maraschino cherry, to decorate

Put some ice cubes into a cocktail shaker with the gin, Maraschino liqueur, and lemon juice. Shake well. Double strain into a chilled Martini glass. Decorate with a maraschino cherry.

Aviation

Fair Lady

lightly beaten egg white
superfine sugar
ice cubes
1 measure gin
4 measures grapefruit juice
1 dash Cointreau

Frost the rim of an old-fashioned glass by dipping it into egg white and pressing it into the sugar. Put some ice cubes into a cocktail shaker and pour the remaining egg white, gin, grapefruit juice, and Cointreau over them. Shake well, then pour into the prepared glass.

Golden Dawn

4–5 ice cubes
juice of ½ orange
1 measure Calvados
1 measure apricot brandy
3 measures gin
soda water, to top up
orange zest strip, to decorate

Put the ice cubes into a cocktail shaker and pour the orange juice, Calvados, apricot brandy, and gin over them. Shake until a frost forms. Strain into a highball glass, top up with soda water, and decorate with an orange zest strip.

Fighting Bob

ice cubes
2 measures gin
½ measure Chartreuse
½ measure cherry brandy
1 teaspoon lemon juice
1 dash Angostura bitters
soda water, to taste

Put some ice cubes into a cocktail shaker and pour the gin, Chartreuse, cherry brandy, lemon juice, and bitters over them. Shake well, pour into a highball glass or tumbler, and add soda water, to taste.

Pink Camellia

ice cubes
2 measures gin
1 measure apricot brandy
2 measures orange juice
2 measures lemon juice
1 measure Campari
1 dash egg white

Fill a cocktail shaker three-quarters full with ice cubes. Add all of the other ingredients, shake well, then strain into a chilled cocktail glass.

Gin Floradora

4–5 ice cubes
1/2 teaspoon sugar syrup
juice of 1/2 lime
1/2 teaspoon grenadine
2 measures gin
dry ginger ale, to top up
lime zest twist, to decorate

Put the ice cubes into a cocktail shaker. Pour the sugar syrup, lime juice, grenadine, and gin over the ice and shake until a frost forms. Pour without straining into a hurricane glass. Top up with dry ginger ale and decorate with a lime zest twist.

Riviera Fizz

ice cubes
1 1/2 measures sloe gin
1/2 measure lemon juice
1/2 measure sugar syrup
Champagne, to top up
lemon zest twist, to decorate

Put some ice cubes into a cocktail shaker with the sloe gin, lemon juice, and sugar syrup and shake well. Strain into a chilled Champagne flute. Top up with Champagne, stir, and decorate with a lemon zest twist.

Riviera Fizz

Tipperary

4–5 ice cubes
juice of 1 lemon
3 measures gin
3 measures dry vermouth

Put the ice cubes into a mixing glass. Pour the lemon juice, gin, and vermouth over the ice. Stir evenly and strain into a chilled cocktail glass.

Alice Springs

4–5 ice cubes
1 measure fresh lemon juice
1 measure fresh orange juice
1/2 teaspoon grenadine
3 measures gin
3 drops Angostura bitters
soda water, to top up
orange slice, to decorate

Put the ice cubes into a cocktail shaker. Pour the fruit juices, grenadine, and gin over the ice. Add the bitters and shake until a frost forms. Pour into a tall glass and top up with soda water. Decorate with an orange slice and serve with straws.

Alice Springs

Berry Collins

4 raspberries, plus extra to decorate
4 blueberries, plus extra to decorate
1 dash strawberry syrup
crushed ice
2 measures gin
2 teaspoons fresh lemon juice
sugar syrup, to taste
soda water, to top up
1 lemon slice, to decorate

Muddle the berries and strawberry syrup in a highball glass, then fill the glass with crushed ice. Add the gin, lemon juice, and sugar syrup. Stir well, then top up with soda water. Decorate with raspberries, blueberries, and a lemon slice.

Tom Collins

2 measures gin
1½ teaspoons lemon juice
1 teaspoon sugar syrup
ice cubes
soda water, to top up
lemon slice, to decorate

Put the gin, lemon juice, and sugar syrup into a tall glass, stir well, and fill the glass with ice. Top up with soda water and decorate with a lemon slice.

Berry Collins

Tom Collins

Gin Garden

Gin Garden

¼ cucumber, peeled and chopped
½ measure elderflower cordial
2 measures gin
1 measure pressed apple juice
ice cubes
peeled cucumber slices, to decorate

Muddle the chopped cucumber and elderflower cordial in a cocktail shaker. Add the gin, apple juice, and some ice cubes and shake well. Double strain into a chilled Martini glass and decorate with cucumber slices.

Maiden's Prayer

ice cubes
2 measures gin
2 measures Cointreau
1 measure orange juice

Fill a cocktail shaker three-quarters full with ice cubes. Pour the gin, Cointreau, and orange juice over the ice and shake well. Strain into a chilled cocktail glass.

Maiden's Blush

ice cubes
2 measures gin
1 measure Pernod
1 teaspoon grenadine

Put some ice cubes into a cocktail shaker and pour the gin, Pernod, and grenadine over them. Shake well and strain into a cocktail glass.

Cherry Julep

3–4 ice cubes, plus finely chopped ice to serve
juice of $1/2$ lemon
1 teaspoon sugar syrup
1 teaspoon grenadine
1 measure cherry brandy
1 measure sloe gin
2 measures gin
lemon zest strips, to decorate

Put the ice cubes into a cocktail shaker. Pour the lemon juice, sugar syrup, grenadine, cherry brandy, sloe gin, and gin over the ice. Shake until a frost forms. Strain into a highball glass filled with chopped ice and decorate with lemon zest strips.

Cherry Julep

Poet's Dream

4–5 ice cubes
1 measure Bénédictine
1 measure dry vermouth
3 measures gin
lemon zest slice

Put the ice cubes into a mixing glass. Pour the Bénédictine, vermouth, and gin over the ice and stir vigorously, without splashing. Strain into a chilled cocktail glass. Twist the lemon zest slice over the drink, then drop it in.

Singapore Sling

ice cubes
1 measure gin
$\frac{1}{2}$ measure cherry brandy
$\frac{1}{4}$ measure Cointreau
$\frac{1}{4}$ measure Bénédictine
$\frac{1}{2}$ measure grenadine
$\frac{1}{2}$ measure lime juice
5 measures pineapple juice
1 dash Angostura bitters
pineapple slice, to decorate
maraschino cherry, to decorate

Put some ice cubes into a cocktail shaker with all the other ingredients and shake well. Strain over more ice cubes in a sling glass. Decorate with a pineapple slice and a cherry impaled on a toothpick.

Singapore Sling

Orange Blossom

4 orange slices, plus extra to decorate
2 teaspoons almond syrup
crushed ice
2 measures gin
1 measure pink grapefruit juice
3 dashes Angostura bitters

Muddle the orange slices and almond syrup in a highball glass. Fill the glass with crushed ice and pour in the gin. Stir, top with the grapefruit juice and bitters, and decorate with extra orange slices. Serve with straws.

Mississippi Mule

ice cubes
1½ measures gin
1 teaspoon crème de cassis
1 teaspoon lemon juice

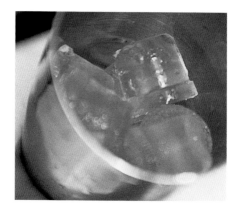

Put some ice cubes into a cocktail
shaker and pour the gin, crème de
cassis, and juice over them. Shake
well, strain into a glass, and add more ice cubes.

Boxcar

caster sugar
ice cubes
1¼ measures Cointreau
1¼ measures gin
1 teaspoon lime juice
1 egg white
1–2 dashes grenadine

Frost the rim of a glass by dipping
it in water and pressing it into the sugar. Put some ice cubes into a cocktail
shaker and pour the Cointreau, gin, lime juice, egg white, and grenadine
over them. Shake very well. Strain the cocktail into the prepared glass.

North Pole

1 measure gin
½ measure lemon juice
½ measure Maraschino liqueur
1 egg white
whipping cream, whipped, to
    decorate

Put the gin, lemon juice,
Maraschino liqueur, and egg white into a cocktail shaker and shake well.
Pour into a cocktail glass and top with whipped cream.

Zed

ice cubes, cracked
1 measure gin
1 measure Mandarine Napoléon
    brandy
3 measures fresh pineapple juice
1 teaspoon sugar
1 lemon slice, cut in half, to
    decorate
mint sprig, to decorate

Put some cracked ice into a cocktail shaker and pour the gin, Mandarine
Napoléon, pineapple juice, and sugar over it. Shake lightly to mix. Pour
into a tall glass and decorate with the half lemon slices and a mint sprig.

Woodstock

2–3 ice cubes, crushed
1 measure gin
1 measure dry vermouth
caster sugar
1/4 measure Cointreau
1 measure fresh orange juice
orange zest
orange slice, to decorate

Put the ice into a cocktail shaker and add the gin, vermouth, Cointreau, and orange juice. Shake to mix, then strain into a chilled cocktail glass. Squeeze the orange zest over the surface and decorate with the orange slice twisted over the rim of the glass.

Hong Kong Sling

ice cubes
1 1/2 measures gin
1/2 measure litchee liqueur
1 measure litchee purée
1 measure lemon juice
1/2 measure sugar syrup
soda water, to top up
fresh litchee in its shell, to decorate

Put some ice cubes into a cocktail shaker. Pour the gin, litchee liqueur and purée, lemon juice, and sugar syrup over them and shake well. Strain over more ice into a sling glass. Stir and top up with soda water. Serve with long straws and a litchee.

Hong Kong Sling

Perfect Lady

ice cubes
2 measures gin
1 measure peach brandy
1 measure lemon juice
1 dash egg white

Fill a mixing glass three-quarters fill with ice cubes. Add the gin, peach brandy, lemon juice, and egg white and stir well. Strain into a chilled cocktail glass.

The Fix

2 measures gin
1 dash pineapple syrup
1 dash fresh lime juice
1 dash fresh lemon juice
1 dash Cointreau
6–8 ice cubes
lemon zest, to decorate
fresh pineapple wedges, to decorate

Put the gin, pineapple syrup, fruit juices and Cointreau into a cocktail shaker and shake well. Strain into an old-fashioned glass over the ice cubes and decorate with the lemon zest and pineapple wedges.

Kiss in the Dark

4–5 ice cubes
1 measure gin
1 measure cherry brandy
1 teaspoon dry vermouth

Put the ice cubes into a cocktail shaker. Pour the gin, cherry brandy, and vermouth over them and shake well. Strain into a chilled cocktail glass.

Gin Fizz

Sloe-ho

Sloe-ho

2 measures sloe gin
1 measure fresh lemon juice
1/2 measure sugar syrup
1/2 measure egg white
ice cubes
soda water, to top up
lemon zest spiral, to decorate

Put the sloe gin, lemon juice, sugar syrup and egg white into a cocktail shaker and shake well. Strain into a highball glass filled with ice cubes and top up with soda water. Decorate with a long lemon zest spiral.

Gin Fizz

ice cubes
2 measures Plymouth gin
1 measure fresh lemon juice
2–3 dashes sugar syrup
1/4 beaten egg white
soda water, to top up
lemon slices, to decorate
mint sprig, to decorate

Put some ice cubes into a cocktail shaker with the gin, lemon juice, sugar syrup, and egg white and shake to mix. Strain into a highball glass and top up with soda water. Decorate with lemon slices and a mint sprig.

Vampire

1 measure dry vermouth
1 measure gin
½ measure lime juice

Put all the ingredients into a cocktail shaker and shake well. Pour into a chilled cocktail glass.

Abbey Road

6 mint leaves, plus extra sprig to decorate
1 piece candied ginger
½ measure fresh lemon juice
2 measures gin
1 measure apple juice
ice cubes, plus crushed ice to serve
lemon wedge, to decorate
mint sprig, to decorate

Muddle the mint leaves, ginger, and lemon juice in a cocktail shaker. Add the gin, apple juice, and some ice cubes and shake well. Strain over crushed ice in an old-fashioned glass and decorate with a lemon wedge and a mint sprig.

Abbey Road

Honeydew

3–4 ice cubes, cracked
1 measure gin
1/2 measure fresh lemon juice
1 dash Pernod
1/3 cup honeydew melon, diced
Champagne, to top up

Put the cracked ice, gin, lemon juice, Pernod, and melon into a food processor or blender and blend for 30 seconds, then pour into a large wine glass. Top up with Champagne.

I love to drink martinis.
Two at the very most.
Three I'm under the table.
Four I'm under the host!

DOROTHY PARKER

Clover Club

ice cubes
juice of 1 lime
$\frac{1}{2}$ teaspoon sugar syrup
1 egg white
3 measures gin
grated lime zest and wedge, to decorate

Put some ice cubes into a cocktail shaker. Pour the lime juice, sugar syrup, egg white, and gin over them and shake to mix. Strain over 5–6 more ice cubes in an old-fashioned glass. Decorate with grated lime zest and a lime wedge.

Night of Passion

6–8 ice cubes
2 measures gin
1 measure Cointreau
1 tablespoon fresh lemon juice
2 measures peach nectar
2 tablespoons passion fruit juice

Put half of the ice cubes into a cocktail shaker with the gin, Cointreau, lemon juice, peach nectar, and passion fruit juice and shake well. Strain over the remaining ice into an old-fashioned glass.

The Doobs Martini

ice cubes
2 teaspoons dry vermouth
2 measures gin
1 measure sloe gin
4 dashes orange bitters
orange zest twist, to decorate

Put some ice cubes into a cocktail shaker. Add the vermouth and shake well, then strain away the excess. Add the gin, sloe gin, and bitters, stir, then strain into a chilled cocktail glass. Decorate with an orange zest twist.

The Doobs Martini

Sloe Gin Sling

1 measure sloe gin
$\frac{1}{2}$ measure lemon juice
soda water, to top up
lemon or orange slice, to decorate
mint sprig, to decorate

Pour the sloe gin and lemon juice into a highball glass. Top up with soda water. Decorate with a lemon or orange slice and a mint sprig.

French Kiss

crushed ice
1 measure gin
1 measure Dubonnet
1 measure dry vermouth
1 maraschino cherry, to decorate

Put some crushed ice into a mixing glass, add the gin, Dubonnet, and vermouth, and stir well. Strain into a cocktail glass and decorate with a maraschino cherry.

Red Lion

ice cubes
1½ measures Grand Marnier
1 tablespoon gin
2 teaspoons orange juice
2 teaspoons lemon juice
lemon zest twist, to decorate

Put some ice cubes into a cocktail shaker and pour the Grand Marnier, gin, and fruit juices over them. Shake well and strain into a glass over more ice cubes. Decorate with a lemon zest twist.

French 75

1 measure gin
juice of ½ lemon
1 teaspoon superfine sugar
chilled Champagne, to top up
lemon slice, to decorate

Put the gin, lemon juice, and sugar into a Champagne saucer and stir well until the sugar has dissolved. Top up with chilled Champagne and decorate with a lemon slice.

French 75

Opal Martini

ice cubes
2 measures gin
1 measure Cointreau
2 measures fresh orange juice
orange zest twist, to decorate

Put some ice cubes into a cocktail shaker with the gin, Cointreau, and orange juice and shake well. Strain into a chilled cocktail glass. Swirl a long orange zest twist in the drink and around the stem of the glass.

Lady of Leisure

ice cubes
1 measure gin
½ measure Chambord
½ measure Cointreau
1 dash fresh lemon juice
1 measure pineapple juice
orange zest strips, to decorate

Put some ice cubes with the gin, Chambord, Cointreau and fruit juices into a cocktail shaker and shake to mix. Strain into a chilled cocktail glass and decorate with orange zest strips.

Gin Sling

4–5 ice cubes
juice of ½ lemon
1 measure cherry brandy
3 measures gin
soda water, to top up
maraschino or fresh sweet cherries, to decorate

Put the ice cubes into a cocktail shaker. Pour the lemon juice, cherry brandy, and gin over the ice. Shake until a frost forms. Pour without straining into a hurricane glass and top up with soda water. Decorate with maraschino or fresh sweet cherries and serve with straws.

Gin Sling

Knockout

4–5 ice cubes
1 measure dry vermouth
½ measure white crème de menthe
2 measures gin
1 drop Pernod
lemon slice, to decorate

Put the ice cubes into a mixing glass. Pour the vermouth, crème de menthe, and gin over the ice, stir vigorously, then strain into a chilled old-fashioned glass. Add the Pernod and serve with a lemon slice.

Do not allow children to mix drinks. It is unseemly and they use too much vermouth.

STEVE ALLEN

Juliana Blue

crushed ice, plus 2–3 ice cubes
1 measure gin
½ measure Cointreau
½ measure blue Curaçao
2 measures pineapple juice
½ measure fresh lime juice
1 measure coconut cream
pineapple wedge, to decorate
maraschino cherries, to decorate

Put some crushed ice into a food processor or blender and pour in the gin, Cointreau, blue Curaçao, fruit juices, and coconut cream. Blend at high speed for several seconds until the mixture has the consistency of soft snow. Strain over ice cubes in a cocktail glass. Decorate with a pineapple wedge and maraschino cherries, impaled on a toothpick.

Red Kiss

3 ice cubes, cracked
1 measure dry vermouth
½ measure gin
½ measure cherry brandy
maraschino cherry, to decorate
lemon zest spiral, to decorate

Put the cracked ice into a mixing glass, add the vermouth, gin, and cherry brandy and stir well. Strain into a chilled cocktail glass and decorate with a maraschino cherry and a lemon zest spiral.

Crossbow

hot cocoa mix
4–5 ice cubes
½ measure gin
½ measure crème de cacao
½ measure Cointreau

Frost the rim of a chilled cocktail glass by dipping it into a little water and pressing it into hot cocoa mix. Put the ice cubes into a cocktail shaker and add the gin, crème de cacao, and Cointreau. Shake vigorously and strain into the prepared glass.

Crossbow

VODKA

Sex on the Beach

ice cubes
1 measure vodka
1 measure peach schnapps
1 measure cranberry juice
1 measure orange juice
1 measure pineapple juice (optional)
orange and lime slices, to decorate

Put some ice cubes into a cocktail shaker and add the vodka, schnapps, cranberry juice, orange juice, and pineapple juice, if using. Shake well. Pour over 3–4 ice cubes in a tall glass, decorate with the orange and lime slices and serve with straws.

Iced Lemon and Mint Vodka

1 tablespoon lemon juice
1 measure lemon cordial
1 measure chilled vodka
ice cubes
tonic water, to top up
mint sprigs, to decorate

Pour the lemon juice, lemon cordial, and vodka into a cocktail shaker and shake well. Pour into a large glass half-filled with ice cubes. Top up with tonic water, add the mint sprigs, and serve immediately.

Iced Lemon and Mint Vodka

Bellini-tini

2 measures vodka
½ measure peach schnapps
2 teaspoons peach juice
Champagne, to top up
peach slices, to decorate

Put the vodka, schnapps, and peach juice into a cocktail shaker and shake
well. Pour into a cocktail glass and top up with Champagne. Decorate
with peach slices.

Harvey Wallbanger

ice cubes
1 measure vodka
3 measures orange juice
1 teaspoon Galliano
orange slices, to decorate

Put some ice cubes into a cocktail shaker and pour the vodka and orange juice over the ice. Shake well for about 10 seconds, then strain into a highball glass filled with ice cubes. Float the Galliano on top. Decorate with orange slices.

Cocktail party: A gathering held to enable forty people to talk about themselves at the same time. The man who remains after the liquor is gone is the host. FRED ALLEN

Warsaw Cocktail

6 ice cubes
1 measure vodka
1/2 measure blackberry-flavored brandy
1/2 measure dry vermouth
1 teaspoon fresh lemon juice

Put the ice cubes into a cocktail shaker and add the vodka, brandy, vermouth, and lemon juice. Shake until a frost forms. Strain into a cocktail glass.

Diamond Ring

1 dash boiling water
1 teaspoon clear honey
3 basil leaves
1 1/2 measures Zubrowka Bison Grass vodka
1 measure pressed apple juice
ice cubes
apple slices, to decorate

Stir the hot water, honey, and basil leaves together in a cocktail shaker until well blended. Add the vodka, apple juice, and some ice cubes. Shake well and double strain into a chilled Martini glass. Decorate with apple slices.

Diamond Ring

Polish Martini

Mudslide

10 ice cubes, cracked
1 measure vodka
1 measure Kahlúa
1 measure Baileys Irish Cream

Put 6 of the cracked ice cubes into a cocktail shaker and add the vodka, Kahlúa, and Baileys. Shake until a frost forms. Strain into a tumbler and add the remaining cracked ice.

Polish Martini

ice cubes
1 measure Zubrowka vodka
1 measure Krupnik vodka
1 measure Wyborowa vodka
1 measure apple juice
lemon zest twist, to decorate

Put the ice cubes into a mixing glass. Pour in the vodkas and the apple juice and stir well. Strain into a chilled cocktail glass and add a lemon zest twist.

Moscow Mule

Screwdriver

Screwdriver

2–3 ice cubes
1½ measures vodka
freshly squeezed orange juice, to top up

Put the ice cubes into a tumbler and pour the vodka over them. Top up
with orange juice and stir lightly.

Moscow Mule

6–8 ice cubes, cracked
2 measures vodka
juice of 2 limes
ginger beer, to top up
lime slice, to decorate
lime zest spiral, to decorate

Put the cracked ice into a highball glass. Add the vodka and lime juice, stir,
and top with ginger beer. Decorate with a lime slice and a lime zest spiral.

New Day

4–5 ice cubes
3 measures vodka
1 measure Calvados
1 measure apricot brandy
juice of ½ orange

Put the ice cubes into a cocktail shaker. Pour the vodka, Calvados, apricot brandy, and orange juice over the ice. Shake until a frost forms. Strain into a sour glass.

Snapdragon

ice cubes
2 measures vodka
4 measures green crème de menthe
soda water, to top up
mint sprig, to decorate

Fill a highball glass with ice cubes. Pour the vodka and crème de menthe over the ice and stir. Top up with soda water. Decorate with a mint sprig.

Snapdragon

Gingersnap

2–3 ice cubes
3 measures vodka
1 measure ginger wine
soda water, to top up

Combine the vodka, ginger wine, and ice in an old-fashioned glass and stir gently. Top up with soda water.

Laila Cocktail

2 lime wedges
2 strawberries, hulled
4 blueberries, plus 3 to decorate
1 dash mango purée
2 measures raspberry vodka
ice cubes

Muddle the lime wedges, berries, and mango purée in a cocktail shaker. Add the vodka with some ice cubes and shake vigorously. Double strain into a chilled Martini glass and garnish with the extra blueberries impaled on a toothpick.

Laila Cocktail

Cosmopolitan

ice cubes
1½ measures citron vodka
1 measure Cointreau
1½ measures cranberry juice
¼ measure fresh lime juice
orange zest twist, flamed (see page 539)

Put the ice cubes into a cocktail shaker, add the vodka, Cointreau,
cranberry juice, and lime juice and shake well. Strain into a chilled cocktail
glass and add a flamed orange zest twist.

Sex in the Dunes

ice cubes
1 measure vodka
1 measure peach schnapps
1/2 measure Chambord raspberry liqueur
1 measure pineapple juice
pineapple strips, to decorate

Put some ice cubes into a cocktail shaker with the vodka, schnapps, Chambord, and pineapple juice. Shake until a frost forms. Strain into an old-fashioned glass filled with ice cubes and decorate with pineapple strips.

Lemon Martini

ice cubes
1½ measures citron vodka
1 measure fresh lemon juice
¼ measure sugar syrup
¼ measure Cointreau
3 drops orange bitters
orange zest twist, to decorate

Put the ice cubes into a cocktail shaker with the vodka, lemon juice, sugar syrup, Cointreau, and bitters and shake well. Strain into a chilled Martini glass and add an orange zest twist.

Illusion

4–6 ice cubes, plus extra to serve
2 measures vodka
½ measure Midori
½ measure Triple Sec
½ measure lime juice
lemonade, to top up
melon slices, to decorate
lemon slices, to decorate
maraschino cherries, to decorate

Put the ice cubes into a cocktail shaker and shake well with the vodka, Midori, Triple Sec, and lime juice. Put more ice cubes into a large hurricane glass and strain the cocktail over the ice. Top up with lemonade, stir, and decorate with melon and lemon slices and maraschino cherries impaled on a toothpick. Serve with long straws.

Illusion

Rising Sun

ice cubes
2 measures vodka
2 teaspoons passion fruit syrup
3 measures grapefruit juice
pink grapefruit slice, to decorate

Put some of the ice cubes into a cocktail shaker with the vodka, passion
fruit syrup, and grapefruit juice and shake to mix. Strain into an old-
fashioned glass over 6–8 ice cubes. Decorate with a pink grapefruit slice.

Flower Power Sour

ice cubes
1½ measures Absolut Mandarin vodka
½ measure Mandarine Napoléon brandy
2 teaspoons elderflower cordial
2 teaspoons sugar syrup
1 measure fresh lemon juice
orange zest, to decorate

Put some ice cubes with the vodka, Mandarine Napoléon, elderflower
cordial, sugar syrup, and lemon juice into a cocktail shaker and shake well.
Strain into an old-fashioned glass filled with ice cubes and decorate with
orange zest.

Rock Chick

ice cubes
1 measure Absolut Kurant vodka
1 dash peach schnapps
1 dash fresh lime juice

Put some ice cubes into a cocktail shaker with all the other ingredients and shake briefly. Strain into a shot glass.

Swallow Dive

ice cubes, plus crushed ice to serve
1 measure honey vodka
1 measure Chambord
1 measure lime juice
4 raspberries, plus 2 to decorate

Put some ice cubes into a cocktail shaker with all the other ingredients. Shake well. Strain over crushed ice in an old-fashioned glass. Top up with more crushed ice and decorate with the 2 extra raspberries.

Swallow Dive

Vodka Gibson

6 ice cubes
1 measure vodka
½ measure dry vermouth
pearl onion, to garnish (optional)

Put the ice cubes into a cocktail shaker and add the vodka and vermouth.
Shake until a frost forms, then strain into a cocktail glass and decorate
with a pearl onion impaled on a toothpick, if you wish.

Oyster Shot

1 small, plump oyster
¾ measure chilled pepper vodka
¾ measure chilled tomato juice
3 drops Tabasco sauce
dash Worcestershire sauce
1 lime wedge, squeezed
pinch of freshly cracked black pepper
pinch of celery salt

Put all the ingredients into a large shot glass in the above order, then slowly tip the entire contents down your throat.

Tokyo Joe

ice cubes
1 measure vodka
1 measure Midori

Put some ice cubes into a cocktail shaker, add the vodka and Midori and shake well. Strain into an old-fashioned glass, over ice cubes if you like.

Vodkatini

1/4 measure dry vermouth
3 measures vodka, chilled in the freezer
1 green olive or lemon zest twist

Swirl the vermouth around a chilled Martini glass, then pour in the vodka. Finish by adding the olive or a lemon zest twist.

Vodkatini

French Leave

ice cubes
1 measure orange juice
1 measure vodka
1 measure Pernod

Put some ice cubes into a cocktail shaker with all the other ingredients and shake well. Strain into a cocktail glass.

Lemon Drop

ice cubes
¾ measure lemon vodka
¾ measure Limoncello lemon liqueur
1 dash fresh lemon juice
1 dash lime cordial

Put some ice cubes into a cocktail shaker with all the other ingredients and shake briefly. Strain into a shot glass.

Lemon Drop

Dragon's Fire

Cool Wind

4–5 ice cubes
1 measure dry vermouth
½ teaspoon Cointreau
3 measures vodka
juice of ½ grapefruit

Put the ice cubes into a mixing glass. Pour the vermouth, Cointreau, vodka, and grapefruit juice over the ice. Stir gently, then strain into a chilled cocktail glass.

Dragon's Fire

ice cubes
1½ measures Absolut Mandarin vodka
1 measure Cointreau
1 dash lime juice
1 measure cranberry juice
orange zest twist, to decorate

Put some ice cubes into a cocktail shaker with the vodka, Cointreau, and fruit juices and shake well. Double strain into a chilled Martini glass. Decorate with an orange zest twist.

Storm at Sea

8–10 ice cubes
2 measures cranberry juice
1 measure pineapple juice
2 teaspoons elderflower cordial
1½ measures Blavod vodka

Put half of the ice cubes with the fruit juices and elderflower cordial into a cocktail shaker and shake well. Strain into an old-fashioned glass over the remaining ice cubes. Slowly add the vodka—it will separate briefly. Serve immediately.

Plasma

ice cubes
2 measures Absolut Peppar vodka
4 measures tomato juice
juice of 1/4 lemon
2 dashes Tabasco sauce
4 dashes Worcestershire sauce
pinch of celery salt
pinch of black pepper
1/2 teaspoon Dijon mustard
1 teaspoon finely chopped dill
cucumber strip, to decorate
seasoned split cherry tomato, to decorate

Put some ice cubes into a cocktail shaker with all the other ingredients. Shake vigorously but briefly, then strain into a highball glass over 6–8 ice cubes. Decorate with a cucumber strip and a seasoned split cherry tomato.

May your glass be ever full,
May the roof over your head be always strong,
And may you be in heaven
Half an hour before the devil knows you're dead.

IRISH DRINKING TOAST

White Spider

2 measures vodka
1 measure clear crème de menthe
crushed ice (optional)

Pour the vodka and crème de menthe into a cocktail shaker. Shake well, then pour into a chilled cocktail glass or over crushed ice.

Xantippe

4–5 ice cubes
1 measure cherry brandy
1 measure yellow Chartreuse
2 measures vodka

Put the ice cubes into a mixing glass. Pour the cherry brandy, Chartreuse, and vodka over the ice and stir vigorously. Strain into a chilled cocktail glass.

Xantippe

Murray Hearn

ice cubes
1½ measures vodka
3 measures orange juice
½ measure Galliano
½ measure Cointreau
1 measure light cream
orange slice, to decorate

Put some ice cubes ino a cocktail shaker and add the vodka, orange juice, Galliano, Cointreau, and cream. Shake well, then strain into a highball glass filled with ice cubes. Decorate with an orange slice.

Fragrance

4–6 ice cubes, plus crushed ice to serve
1½ measures vodka
½ measure Midori melon liqueur
1 measure lemon juice
1 measure pineapple juice
1 dash sugar syrup
1 lemon wedge

Put the ice cubes with the vodka, Midori, fruit juices, and sugar syrup into a cocktail shaker and shake. Strain into a highball glass filled with crushed ice. Squeeze the lemon wedge over the drink, drop it in, and serve with straws.

Fragrance

Chocotini

cocoa powder
ice cubes
2 measures vodka
1 measure dark crème de cacao
¼ measure sugar syrup
½ measure chocolate syrup

Frost a chilled Martini glass by dipping the rim into water, then pressing it into cocoa powder. Put the ice cubes into a cocktail shaker, add the vodka, crème de cacao, sugar syrup, and chocolate syrup and shake well. Strain into the prepared glass.

White Russian

6 ice cubes, cracked
1 measure vodka
1 measure Tia Maria
1 measure milk or heavy cream

Put half of the ice into a cocktail shaker and add the vodka, Tia Maria, and milk or cream. Shake until a frost forms. Put the remaining ice in a tall, narrow glass and strain the cocktail over it.

White Russian

Watermelon Martini

One of Those

1 measure vodka
4 measures cranberry juice
2 dashes Amaretto di Saronno liqueur
juice of 1/2 lime
ice cubes
lime slice, to decorate

Pour the vodka, cranberry juice, Amaretto di Saronno, and lime juice into a cocktail shaker and shake well. Pour into a highball glass half-filled with ice cubes and decorate with a lime slice.

Watermelon Martini

ice cubes
1 lime wedge
4 watermelon chunks
1 1/2 measures vodka
1/2 measure passion fruit liqueur
1 dash cranberry juice
watermelon wedge, to decorate

Squeeze the lime wedge into a cocktail shaker, add some ice cubes, the watermelon chunks, vodka, passion fruit liqueur, and cranberry juice, and shake well. Double strain into a chilled Martini glass and decorate with a watermelon wedge impaled on a toothpick.

Godmother

2–3 ice cubes, cracked
1½ measures vodka
½ measure Amaretto di Saronno liqueur

Put the cracked ice into a tumbler. Add the vodka and Amaretto di Saronno and stir lightly.

Apple Martini

ice cubes
2 measures vodka
1 measure apple schnapps
1 tablespoon apple purée
1 dash lime juice
pinch of ground cinnamon
red apple wedges, to decorate

Put some ice cubes into a cocktail shaker with the vodka, schnapps, apple purée, lime juice, and cinnamon and shake well. Double strain into a chilled Martini glass. Decorate with red apple wedges.

Apple Martini

Cape Codder

ice cubes
2 measures vodka
4 measures cranberry juice
6 lime wedges

Fill a highball glass with ice cubes. Pour the vodka and cranberry juice over the ice. Squeeze 3 of the lime wedges into the drink. Stir well, decorate with the remaining lime wedges, and serve with a straw.

Dark Knight

ice cubes
1 measure Kahlúa
1 measure vodka
1 measure cold espresso coffee
2 teaspoons sugar syrup

Put some ice cubes into a cocktail shaker with the Kahlúa, vodka, coffee, and sugar syrup and shake well. Strain into a chilled Martini glass and serve.

Beer is not a good cocktail-party drink, especially in a home where you don't know where the bathroom is. BILLY CARTER

Kurant Blush

PDQ

4–5 ice cubes
1½ measures chilli-flavored vodka
1 measure vodka
2 measures chilled beef stock
1 tablespoon fresh lemon juice
1 dash Tabasco sauce
1 dash Worcestershire sauce
salt and black pepper
lemon slice, to decorate
chilli, to decorate

Put the ice cubes into a cocktail shaker. Pour the vodkas, stock, lemon juice, and Tabasco and Worcestershire sauces over the ice. Shake until a frost forms. Strain into a hurricane glass. Season to taste with salt and pepper and decorate with a lemon slice and a chilli.

Kurant Blush

ice cubes
1½ measures Absolut Kurant vodka
½ measure fraise liqueur
1 measure cranberry juice
2 lime wedges
redcurrant, to decorate

Put some ice cubes into a cocktail shaker with all the other ingredients and shake well. Double strain into a chilled Martini glass and decorate with a redcurrant impaled on a toothpick.

Katinka

ice cubes
1½ measures vodka
1 measure apricot brandy
2 teaspoons fresh lime juice
mint sprig, to decorate

Put some ice cubes into a cocktail shaker and all the other ingredients and shake well. Strain into a cocktail glass and decorate with a mint sprig.

Decatini

ice cubes
2 measures raspberry vodka
½ measure chocolate syrup, plus extra to decorate
1 measure sour cherry purée
½ measure heavy cream

Fill a cocktail shaker with ice cubes and add the vodka, chocolate syrup and half of the cream. Shake well and strain into a chilled Martini glass. Shake the sour cherry purée with the remaining cream in a clean shaker. Slowly pour the cherry liquid onto a spoon that is held in contact with the chocolate liquid in the glass; this will produce a layering effect. Decorate with a "swirl" of chocolate syrup.

Decatini

Le Mans

2–3 ice cubes, cracked
1 measure Cointreau
$\frac{1}{2}$ measure vodka
soda water, to top up
lemon slice, to decorate

Put the cracked ice into a tall glass. Add the Cointreau and vodka, stir, and top up with soda water. Float a lemon slice on top of the drink for decoration.

Sea Breeze

ice cubes
2 measures vodka
4 measures cranberry juice
2 measures pink grapefruit juice
2 lime wedges

Fill a highball glass with ice cubes. Pour the vodka and fruit juices over the ice. Squeeze the lime wedges over the drink and stir lightly.

Sea Breeze

Iceberg

4–6 ice cubes
1½ measures vodka
1 dash Pernod

Put the ice cubes into an old-fashioned glass. Pour the vodka over the ice and add the Pernod.

Astronaut

8–10 ice cubes, cracked
½ measure white rum
½ measure vodka
½ measure fresh lemon juice
1 dash passion fruit juice
lemon wedge, to decorate

Put half of the cracked ice into a cocktail shaker and add the rum, vodka, and juices. Shake until a frost forms. Strain it into an old-fashioned glass filled with the remaining ice. Decorate with a lemon wedge.

Astronaut

Vodka Sazerac

Yokohama

4–5 ice cubes
3 measures vodka
3 drops Pernod
juice of 1 orange
1/2 teaspoon grenadine

Put the ice cubes into a cocktail shaker. Pour the vodka, Pernod, orange juice, and grenadine over the ice. Shake until a frost forms. Strain into a chilled cocktail glass.

Vodka Sazerac

1 sugar cube
2 drops Angostura bitters
3 drops Pernod
2–3 ice cubes
2 measures vodka
lemonade, to top up

Put the sugar cube in an old-fashioned glass and shake the bitters on to it. Add the Pernod and swirl it around to coat the inside of the glass. Drop in the ice cubes and pour in the vodka. Top up with lemonade and stir gently.

Blue Moon

5–6 ice cubes, cracked
¾ measure vodka
¾ measure tequila
1 measure blue Curaçao
lemonade, to top up

Put half of the cracked ice into a mixing glass. Add the vodka, tequila, and blue Curaçao and stir to mix. Put the remaining ice into a tall glass and strain in the cocktail over it. Top up with lemonade and serve with a straw.

Basil's Mango Sling

ice cubes, plus crushed ice
1½ measures vodka
1½ measures mango purée
1 measure apricot liqueur
½ measure lemon juice
1 dash sugar syrup
soda water, to top up
mango slices, to decorate

Put some ice cubes with the vodka, mango purée, apricot liqueur, lemon juice, and sugar syrup into a cocktail shaker and add some ice cubes and shake very briefly. Strain into a sling glass filled with crushed ice. Top up with soda water and decorate with mango slices.

Basil's Mango Sling

Hair Raiser

1–2 ice cubes, cracked
1 measure vodka
1 measure sweet vermouth
1 measure tonic water
lemon and lime zest spirals, to decorate

Put the cracked ice into a tall glass and pour the vodka, vermouth, and tonic water over it. Stir lightly. Decorate with the lemon and lime zest spirals and serve with a straw.

Pillow Talk

$1/2$ measure chilled strawberry vodka
$1/2$ measure Mozart white chocolate liqueur
1 dash aerosol cream

Pour the chilled vodka into a shot glass. Using the back of a bar spoon, slowly float the chocolate liqueur over the vodka. Top with the cream.

Pillow Talk

Vodka Collins

6 ice cubes
2 measures vodka
juice of 1 lime
1 teaspoon superfine sugar
soda water, to top up
lemon or lime slice, to decorate
maraschino cherry, to decorate

Put half of the ice cubes into a cocktail shaker and add the vodka, lime juice, and sugar. Shake until a frost forms. Strain into a large tumbler, add the remaining ice, and top up with soda water. Decorate with a slice of lemon or lime and a maraschino cherry.

Haven

ice cubes
1 tablespoon grenadine
1 measure Pernod
1 measure vodka
soda water, to top up

Put 2–3 ice cubes in an old-fashioned glass. Dash the grenadine over the ice, then pour in the Pernod and vodka. Top up with soda water.

Haven

Machete

ice cubes
1 measure vodka
2 measures pineapple juice
3 measures tonic water

Fill a tall glass or wine glass with ice cubes. Pour the vodka, pineapple juice, and tonic water into a mixing glass. Stir, then pour the mixture over the ice cubes in the glass.

Vocachino

ice cubes
2 measures vodka
1/2 measure Kahlúa
1/2 measure cold espresso coffee
1/2 measure light cream
1 dash sugar syrup
1/2 teaspoon cocoa

Put the ice cubes into a cocktail shaker and add the vodka, Kahlúa, coffee, cream, sugar syrup, and cocoa. Shake briefly then strain into shot glasses. Serves 4

Vocachino

Combined Forces

4–5 ice cubes
2 measures vodka
1 measure dry vermouth
1/2 teaspoon Triple Sec
juice of 1/2 fresh lemon

Put the ice cubes into a mixing glass. Add all the other ingredients, stir vigorously, then strain into a chilled cocktail glass.

White Leopard

4–5 ice cubes
2 measures vodka
1 measure Grand Marnier
juice of 1/2 orange
juice of 1/2 lemon

Put the ice cubes into a cocktail shaker. Pour the vodka, Grand Marnier, and fruit juices over the ice. Shake until a frost forms. Strain into a sour glass.

Inspiration

4–5 ice cubes
½ measure Bénédictine
½ measure dry vermouth
2 measures vodka
lime zest spiral, to decorate

Put the ice cubes into a mixing glass. Pour the Bénédictine, vermouth, and vodka over the ice. Stir vigorously, then strain into a chilled cocktail glass and decorate with the lime zest spiral.

Lemon Grass Collins

crushed ice
2 measures lemon grass vodka
½ measure vanilla liqueur
1 dash lemon juice
1 dash sugar syrup
ginger beer, to top up
lemon slices, to decorate

Fill a large Collins glass with crushed ice. Pour, in order, the vodka, vanilla liqueur, lemon juice, and sugar syrup over the ice. Stir, add more ice and top up with ginger beer. Decorate with lemon slices and serve with long straws.

Lemon Grass Collins

Purple Haze

ice cubes
1 measure vodka
1 dash Cointreau
1 dash fresh lemon juice
1 dash Chambord raspberry liqueur

Put some ice cubes into a cocktail shaker with the vodka, Cointreau and lemon juice and shake briefly. Strain into a shot glass. Add the dash of Chambord slowly at the end: this will settle towards the bottom of the drink.

The whole world is drunk and we're just the cocktail of the moment. Someday soon, the world will wake up, down two aspirin with a glass of tomato juice, and wonder what the hell all the fuss was about.

DEAN MARTIN – THE RAT PACK

Bay Breeze

Green Island Quiet Sunday

4–6 ice cubes, plus crushed ice to serve
1 measure vodka
4 measures orange juice
3 dashes Amaretto di Saronno liqueur
few drops of grenadine

Put the ice cubes into a cocktail shaker with the vodka, orange juice, and Amaretto di Saronno and shake well. Strain into a highball glass filled with crushed ice, then add a few drops of grenadine.

Bay Breeze

ice cubes
4 measures cranberry juice
2 measures vodka
2 measures pineapple juice
lime wedges, to decorate

Fill a highball glass with ice cubes and pour in the cranberry juice. Pour the vodka and pineapple juice into a chilled cocktail shaker. Shake well, then pour gently over the cranberry juice. Decorate with lime wedges and serve with long straws.

Marguerite

4–5 ice cubes, plus cracked ice to serve
3 measures vodka
juice of 1 lemon
juice of ½ orange
raspberry syrup, Maraschino liqueur, or grenadine, to taste

Put the ice cubes into a cocktail shaker. Pour the vodka, fruit juices, and raspberry syrup, Maraschino liqueur, or grenadine over the ice. Shake until a frost forms. Strain into an old-fashioned glass filled with cracked ice.

Strawberry Fields

1 lime wedge
1 dash strawberry syrup
1 strawberry, hulled
1 measure Absolut Kurant vodka
ice cubes

Muddle the lime wedge, syrup, and strawberry in a cocktail shaker, add the vodka and some ice cubes, and shake briefly. Strain into a shot glass.

Strawberry Fields

Black Russian

ice cubes, cracked
2 measures vodka
1 measure Kahlúa
chocolate stick, to decorate (optional)

Put some cracked ice into a mixing glass. Add the vodka and Kahlúa and stir. Pour into a short glass without straining. Decorate with a chocolate stick, if you like.

Bloody Mary

4–5 ice cubes
juice of 1/2 lemon
1/2 teaspoon horseradish sauce
2 drops Worcestershire sauce
1 drop Tabasco sauce
2 measures thick tomato juice
2 measures vodka
pinch of salt
pinch of cayenne pepper
celery stick, with the leaves left on, to decorate

Put the ice cubes into a cocktail shaker. Pour the lemon juice, horseradish, Worcestershire and Tabasco sauces, tomato juice, and vodka over the ice. Shake until a frost forms. Pour into a tall glass and add the salt and cayenne pepper. Decorate with a celery stick.

Road Runner

6 ice cubes, cracked
2 measures vodka
1 measure Amaretto di Saronno liqueur
1 measure coconut milk
grated nutmeg, to decorate

Put the cracked ice into a cocktail shaker and add the vodka, Amaretto di Saronno, and coconut milk. Shake until a frost forms, then strain into a cocktail glass. Sprinkle with a pinch of freshly grated nutmeg.

Vodka Sour

4–5 ice cubes
2 measures vodka
½ measure sugar syrup
1 egg white
1½ measures fresh lemon juice
3 drops Angostura bitters, to decorate

Put the ice cubes into a cocktail shaker, add the vodka, sugar syrup, egg white, and lemon juice and shake until a frost forms. Pour without straining into a cocktail glass and shake the Angostura bitters on the top to decorate.

Vodka Sour

Surf Rider

4–5 ice cubes
3 measures vodka
1 measure sweet vermouth
juice of 1/2 lemon
juice of 1 orange
1/2 teaspoon grenadine

Put the ice cubes into a cocktail shaker. Pour the vodka, vermouth, fruit juices, and grenadine over the ice. Shake until a frost forms. Strain into a sour glass.

The Glamor Martini

ice cubes
11/2 measures vodka
1/2 measure cherry brandy
2 measures blood orange juice
1/2 measure lime juice
orange zest twist, to decorate

Put some ice cubes into a cocktail shaker with all the other ingredients and shake well. Strain into a chilled Martini glass. Decorate with an orange zest twist.

The Glamor Martini

Vesper

ice cubes
3 measures gin
1 measure vodka
½ measure Lillet apéritif wine
lemon zest twist, to decorate

Put the ice cubes into a cocktail shaker with the gin, vodka, and Lillet and shake well. Strain into a chilled cocktail glass and add a lemon zest twist.

Valentine Martini

ice cubes
2 measures raspberry vodka
6 raspberries, plus 2 to decorate
½ measure lime juice
1 dash sugar syrup
lime zest twist, to decorate

Put some ice cubes into a cocktail shaker with the vodka, raspberries, lime juice, and sugar syrup and shake well. Double strain into a chilled Martini glass. Decorate with the extra raspberries impaled on a toothpick and a lime zest twist.

Valentine Martini

Razzmopolitan

Legal High

1 dash Amaretto di Saronno liqueur
1 pink grapefruit wedge
1 measure Vod-Ca (hemp vodka)
ice cubes

Muddle the Amaretto di Saronno and grapefruit in the base of a shaker. Add the vodka and a few ice cubes and shake briefly. Strain into a shot glass.

Razzmopolitan

1½ measures Stoli Razberi vodka
1 measure Cointreau
1 dash lime juice
1 measure cranberry juice
4 raspberries, plus 2 to decorate

Put the vodka, Cointreau, fruit juices, and raspberries into a cocktail shaker and shake well. Double strain into a chilled Martini glass and decorate with the extra raspberries impaled on a toothpick.

October Revolution

5–6 ice cubes, cracked
1 measure vodka
1 measure Tia Maria
1 measure crème de cacao
1 measure double cream

Put half of the cracked ice into a cocktail shaker. Pour the vodka, Tia Maria, crème de cacao, and cream over the ice and shake until a frost forms. Put the remaining ice into a tall, narrow glass, strain the cocktail over the ice, and serve with a straw.

Blackberry Martini

2 measures Absolut Kurant vodka
1 measure crème de mure
ice cubes
blackberry, to decorate

Put the vodka and crème de mure into a mixing glass, add some ice cubes, and stir well. Strain into a chilled Martini glass and decorate with a single blackberry impaled on a toothpick.

Blackberry Martini

Parrot's Head Punch

ice cubes
1¹/₂ measures vodka
1 measure passion fruit liqueur
2 measures watermelon juice
1 measure cranberry juice
1¹/₂ measures pink grapefruit juice
grapefruit slices, to decorate

Fill a hurricane glass with ice cubes. Pour the ingredients, one by one and in order over the ice. Decorate with grapefruit slices and serve with long straws.

Melon Ball

5 ice cubes, cracked
1 measure vodka
1 measure Midori melon liqueur
1 measure orange juice, plus extra for topping up (optional)
orange slice, to decorate
banana ball, to decorate

Put the cracked ice into a tall glass or goblet. Pour the vodka, Midori, and orange juice into a cocktail shaker. Shake well, then strain into the glass. Top up with more orange juice, if necessary. Decorate with an orange slice and a banana ball and serve with a straw.

Let us candidly admit that there are shameful blemishes on the American past, of which the worst by far is rum. Nevertheless, we have improved man's lot and enriched his civilization with rye, bourbon and the Martini cocktail. In all history has any other nation done so much?

BERNARD DE VOTO

WHISKEY

Rhett Butler

4–5 ice cubes, plus extra to serve
2 measures bourbon whiskey
4 measures cranberry juice
2 tablespoons sugar syrup
1 tablespoon fresh lime juice
lime slices, to decorate

Put the ice cubes into a cocktail shaker with the bourbon, cranberry juice, sugar syrup, and lime juice and shake well. Fill an old-fashioned glass with ice cubes and strain the cocktail over them. Decorate with lime slices and serve with straws.

Big Buff

1 strawberry, hulled
3 raspberries
3 blueberries, plus extra to decorate
2 teaspoons Chambord raspberry liqueur
1 dash fresh lime juice
2 measures Buffalo Trace bourbon whiskey
3 measures cranberry juice
4–5 ice cubes

Muddle the berries and Chambord in a cocktail shaker. Add the lime juice, bourbon, cranberry juice, and ice cubes. Shake, then pour without straining into a highball glass and decorate with blueberries.

Rhett Butler

Big Buff

Bourbon Fixed

ice cubes
2 measures bourbon whiskey
1 measure sour cherry purée
1 tablespoon fresh lime juice
2 teaspoons sugar syrup
lime zest spirals, to decorate

Put some ice cubes into a cocktail shaker with the bourbon, cherry purée, lime juice, and sugar syrup and shake to mix. Strain into an old-fashioned glass filled with ice cubes and decorate with lime zest spirals.

Capricorn

4–5 ice cubes, cracked
1 measure bourbon whiskey
1/2 measure apricot brandy
1/2 measure lemon juice
2 measures orange juice
orange slice, to decorate

Put half of the cracked ice cubes into a cocktail shaker and add the whiskey, apricot brandy, and fruit juices. Shake to mix. Put the remaining ice cubes into an old-fashioned glass and strain the cocktail over them. Decorate with an orange slice.

Rickey

4–5 ice cubes
1 1/2 measures whiskey
1 1/2 measures lime juice
soda water, to top up
lime zest twist, to decorate

Put the ice cubes into a tall glass with the whiskey and the lime juice. Top up with soda water and stir. Garnish with a lime zest twist.

Tar

4–5 ice cubes
juice of 1 lemon
1/2 teaspoon grenadine
1 measure crème de cacao
3 measures whiskey

Put the ice cubes into a cocktail shaker. Pour in the lemon juice, grenadine, crème de cacao, and whiskey and shake until a frost forms. Strain into a chilled cocktail glass. Serve with a straw.

Benedict

3–4 ice cubes
1 measure Bénédictine
3 measures whiskey
dry ginger ale, to top up

Put the ice cubes into a mixing glass. Pour the Bénédictine and whiskey over the ice. Stir evenly without splashing. Pour without straining into a chilled highball glass. Top up with dry ginger ale.

Benedict

Mint Julep I

10 mint leaves
1 teaspoon sugar syrup
4 dashes Angostura bitters
crushed ice
2 measures bourbon whiskey
mint sprig, to decorate

Muddle the mint leaves, sugar syrup, and bitters in a highball glass. Fill the glass with crushed ice, then add the bourbon. Stir well and decorate with a mint sprig.

Mint Julep II

3 sprigs mint, plus extra to decorate
½ tablespoon superfine sugar
1 tablespoon soda water
2–3 ice cubes
1 measure bourbon whiskey

Crush the mint with the superfine sugar in an old-fashioned glass or large tumbler and rub it around the insides of the glass. Discard the mint. Dissolve the sugar in the soda water, add the ice, and pour the Bourbon over it. Do not stir. Decorate with the extra sprig of mint.

Cliquet

4–5 ice cubes
juice of 1 orange
3 measures bourbon or Scotch whiskey
1 tablespoon dark rum

Put the ice cubes into a mixing glass. Pour the orange juice, whiskey and rum over the ice. Stir vigorously, then strain into a sour glass.

Always do sober what you said you'd do drunk. That will teach you to keep your mouth shut. ERNEST HEMINGWAY

Algonquin

4–5 ice cubes
1 measure pineapple juice
1 measure dry vermouth
3 measures bourbon or Scotch whiskey

Put the ice cubes into a mixing glass. Pour the pineapple juice, vermouth, and whiskey over the ice. Stir vigorously until nearly frothy, then strain into a chilled cocktail glass. Decorate with a cocktail umbrella and a straw, if you like.

Early Night

1 tablespoon fresh lemon juice
1 measure clear honey
1 measure whiskey
2 measures boiling water
1 measure ginger wine
lemon slice, to decorate

Put the lemon juice and honey into a toddy glass and stir well. Add the whiskey and continue stirring. Stir in the boiling water, then add the ginger wine. Decorate with a lemon slice. Stir continuously while drinking it hot.

Whiskey Mac

3–4 ice cubes
1 measure Scotch whiskey
1 measure ginger wine

Put the ice cubes into an old-fashioned glass. Pour the whiskey and ginger wine over the ice and stir slightly.

Early Night

Whiskey Mac

Bourbon Peach Smash

Bourbon Peach Smash

6 mint leaves
3 peach slices
3 lemon slices, plus 1 extra to decorate
2 teaspoons superfine sugar
2 measures bourbon whiskey
ice cubes, plus crushed ice to serve
mint sprig, to decorate

Muddle the mint leaves, peach slice, 3 lemon slices, and sugar in a cocktail shaker. Add the bourbon and some ice cubes and shake well. Strain over crushed ice in an old-fashioned glass. Decorate with a mint sprig and the extra lemon slice and serve with short straws.

Canadian Daisy

4–5 ice cubes, plus extra to serve
2 measures Canadian whiskey
2 teaspoons lemon juice
1 teaspoon raspberry juice
1 teaspoon sugar syrup
soda water, to top up
whole raspberries, to decorate
1 teaspoon brandy

Put the ice cubes into a cocktail shaker with the whiskey, fruit juices, and sugar syrup and shake well. Strain into a tall glass. Add ice and top up with soda water. Decorate with raspberries and float the brandy on top of the drink.

Black Jack

¾ measure Jack Daniel's
¾ measure black Sambuca

Pour the Jack Daniel's into a shot glass. Using the back of a bar spoon, slowly float the Sambuca over the Jack Daniel's.

Rollin' Stoned

4–5 ice cubes, plus extra to serve
2 measures Thai whiskey
1 dash banana liqueur
1 dash raspberry liqueur
1 dash lime juice
2 measures orange juice
2 measures pineapple juice
oranges slices, to decorate
maraschino cherries, to decorate

Put all the ingredients into a cocktail shaker. Shake and strain into a highball glass filled with ice cubes. Decorate with orange slices and maraschino cherries and serve with long straws.

Rollin' Stoned

Whizz Bang

4–5 ice cubes
3 drops orange bitters
½ teaspoon grenadine
1 measure dry vermouth
3 measures Scotch whiskey
1 drop Pernod

Put the ice cubes into a mixing glass. Shake the bitters over the ice and pour in the grenadine, vermouth, and whiskey. Stir vigorously, then strain into a chilled cocktail glass. Add the Pernod and stir.

Virginia Mint Julep

9 young mint sprigs, plus extra to decorate
1 teaspoon sugar syrup
crushed ice
3 measures bourbon whiskey

Muddle the mint and sugar syrup in an iced silver mug or tall glass. Fill the mug or glass with crushed ice, pour the bourbon over the ice, and stir gently. Pack in more crushed ice and stir until a frost forms. Wrap the mug or glass in a table napkin and decorate with a mint sprig.

Virginia Mint Julep

Godfather

ice cubes
2 measures J&B Rare Scotch whiskey
1 measure Amaretto di Saronno liqueur

Put some ice cubes into a cocktail shaker with the whiskey and Amaretto di Saronno and shake vigorously. Strain into a small old-fashioned glass filled with ice cubes.

Italian Heather

4–5 ice cubes
4 measures Scotch whiskey
1 measure Galliano
lemon zest twist, to decorate

Put the ice cubes into a tall glass and stir in the whiskey and Galliano. Decorate with a lemon zest twist.

Leprechaun Dancer

4–5 ice cubes
1 measure Irish whiskey
1 measure lemon juice
soda water, to top up
dry ginger ale, to top up
lemon zest twist, to decorate

Combine the ice cubes, whiskey, and lemon juice in a highball glass. Top up with equal measures of soda water and dry ginger ale. Decorate with a lemon zest twist.

Rob Roy

1 ice cube, cracked
1 measure Scotch whiskey
1/2 measure vermouth
1 dash Angostura bitters
lemon zest spiral, to decorate

Put the cracked ice, whiskey, vermouth, and bitters into a mixing glass and stir well. Strain into a cocktail glass and decorate the rim with a lemon zest spiral.

Bobby Burns

4–5 cubes
1 measure Scotch whiskey
1 measure dry vermouth
1 tablespoon Bénédictine
lemon zest strip, to decorate

Put the ice cubes into a cocktail shaker with the whiskey, vermouth, and
Bénédictine and shake until a frost forms. Strain into a chilled cocktail
glass and decorate with a lemon zest strip.

*Never trust any complicated cocktail
that remains perfectly clear until the
last ingredient goes in, and then
immediately clouds.* TERRY PRACHETT

Roamin' the Gloamin'

4–5 ice cubes
2 measures Scotch whiskey
1 measure Cointreau
2 tablespoons fresh orange juice
orange slice, to decorate

Put the ice cubes into a cocktail shaker. Add the whiskey, Cointreau, and orange juice and shake until a frost forms. Pour into an old-fashioned glass and decorate with an orange slice.

For art to exist, for any sort of aesthetic activity or perception to exist, a certain physiological precondition is indispensable: intoxication.   FRIEDRICH NIETZSCHE

Rattlesnake

4–5 ice cubes, plus extra to serve
1½ measures whiskey
1 teaspoon lemon juice
1 teaspoon sugar syrup
1 egg white
few drops Pernod

Put all the ingredients into a cocktail shaker and shake very well. Strain into a glass and add more ice.

Drinking is a way of ending the day.

ERNEST HEMINGWAY

Eclipse

4–5 ice cubes
2 measures Jack Daniel's
½ measure Chambord raspberry liqueur
½ measure lime juice
1 dash sugar syrup
1 measure cranberry juice
1 measure raspberry juice
raspberry, to decorate
lime wedge, to decorate

Put the ice cubes into a cocktail shaker with the other ingredients and shake well. Strain into a large highball glass filled with crushed ice. Serve with long straws and decorate with a raspberry and a lime wedge.

An alcoholic is someone you don't like who drinks as much as you do. DYLAN THOMAS

Blinker

cracked ice cubes
$1/2$ measure Canadian whiskey
$3/4$ measure grapefruit juice
$1/4$ measure grenadine

Put some cracked ice into a cocktail shaker with the whiskey, grapefruit juice, and grenadine and shake well. Serve in a chilled cocktail glass.

❝ I'd rather have a bottle in front of me, than a frontal lobotomy. ❞ TOM WAITS

St Clement's Manhattan

ice cubes
1 measure orange-infused bourbon whiskey
1 measure lemon-infused bourbon whiskey
1 tablespoon sweet vermouth
4 dashes Angostura bitters
orange and lemon zest twists, to decorate

Put the ice cubes into a mixing glass with the whiskeys, vermouth, and bitters and stir well. Strain into a chilled cocktail glass and decorate with orange and lemon zest twists.

Golden Daisy

4–5 ice cubes
juice of 1 lemon
1 teaspoon sugar syrup
1/2 measure Cointreau
3 measures whiskey
lime wedge, to decorate

Put the ice cubes into a cocktail shaker. Pour the lemon juice, sugar syrup, Cointreau, and whiskey over the ice and shake until a frost forms. Strain into an old-fashioned glass and decorate with a lime wedge.

Southerly Buster

4–5 ice cubes
1 measure blue Curaçao
3 measures whiskey
lemon zest strip, to decorate

Put the ice cubes into a mixing glass. Pour the Curaçao and whiskey over the ice, stir vigorously, then strain into a chilled cocktail glass. Twist the lemon zest strip over the drink and drop it in. Serve with a straw.

Southerly Buster

Zoom

ice cubes
2 measures Scotch whiskey
1 teaspoon clear honey
1 measure chilled water
1 measure light cream

Put the ice cubes into a cocktail shaker, add the whiskey, honey, chilled water, and cream and shake well. Strain into an old-fashioned glass and serve at once.

Nerida

4–5 ice cubes
juice of ½ lime or lemon
3 measures Scotch whiskey
dry ginger ale, to top up
lime or lemon slices, to decorate

Put the ice cubes, lime or lemon juice, and whiskey into a cocktail shaker and shake until a frost forms. Pour without straining into a chilled Collins glass. Top up with dry ginger ale and stir gently. Decorate with lime or lemon slices.

The problem with the world is that everyone is a few drinks behind. HUMPHREY BOGART

Silky Pin

Rusty Nail

Silky Pin

ice cubes
1 measure Scotch whiskey
1 measure Drambuie Cream Liqueur

Fill an old-fashioned glass with ice cubes and pour the Scotch whiskey and Drambuie Cream Liqueur over them. Stir gently.

Rusty Nail

ice cubes
$1\frac{1}{2}$ measures Scotch whiskey
1 measure Drambuie

Fill an old-fashioned glass with ice cubes and pour the Scotch whiskey and Drambuie over them. Stir gently.

American Belle

1/2 measure cherry liqueur
1/2 measure Amaretto di Saronno liqueur
1/2 measure bourbon whiskey

Pour the cherry liqueur into a shot glass. Using the back of a bar spoon, slowly float the Amaretto de Saronno over the cherry liqueur. Float the bourbon over the Amaretto in the same way.

I'll admit I may have seen better days . . . but I'm still not to be had for the price of a cocktail, like a salted peanut.

BETTE DAVIS

Barbera

5 ice cubes, cracked
1 measure bourbon whiskey
3/4 measure Drambuie
1/4 measure Amaretto di Saronno
2 dashes orange bitters
lemon zest twist
orange slice, to decorate

Put half of the ice into a mixing glass with the whiskey, liqueurs, and bitters. Put the remaining ice in a tumbler and strain the cocktail over it. Squeeze the lemon zest over the surface and decorate with an orange slice.

A Kiwi in Tennessee

Lynchburg Lemonade

A Kiwi in Tennessee

¹/₂ kiwifruit, peeled
2 measures Jack Daniel's
1 measure kiwifruit schnapps
1 measure fresh lemon juice
ice cubes
lemonade, to top up
kiwifruit slices, to decorate

Muddle the kiwifruit in a cocktail shaker, then add the Jack Daniel's, schnapps, and lemon juice. Add some ice cubes and shake well. Strain into a highball glass filled with ice cubes. Stir and top up with lemonade. Decorate with kiwifruit slices.

Lynchburg Lemonade

ice cubes
1¹/₂ measures Jack Daniel's
1 measure Cointreau
1 measure fresh lemon juice
lemonade, to top up
lemon slices, to decorate

Put some ice cubes with the Jack Daniel's, Cointreau, and lemon juice into a cocktail shaker and shake well. Strain into a highball glass filled with ice cubes. Top up with lemonade and stir. Decorate with lemon slices.

Club

3 ice cubes, cracked
2 dashes Angostura bitters
1 measure Scotch whiskey
1 dash grenadine
lemon zest spiral, to decorate
maraschino cherry, to decorate

Put the ice into a mixing glass. Add the bitters, whiskey, and grenadine and stir well. Strain into a cocktail glass and decorate with a lemon zest spiral and a maraschino cherry.

Boomerang

$\frac{1}{2}$ measure Jagermeister
$\frac{1}{2}$ measure bourbon whiskey

Pour the Jagermeister into a shot glass. Using the back of a bar spoon, slowly float the bourbon over the Jagermeister.

Boomerang

Aberdeen Angus

2 measures Scotch whiskey
1 measure Drambuie
1 teaspoon clear honey
2 teaspoons lime juice

Combine the whiskey and the honey in a mug and stir until smooth. Add the lime juice. Warm the Drambuie in a small saucepan over a low heat. Pour into a ladle, ignite, and pour into the mug. Stir and serve immediately.

Mike Collins

5–6 ice cubes
juice of 1 lemon
1 tablespoon sugar syrup
3 measures Irish whiskey
orange slice
maraschino cherry
soda water, to top up
orange zest spiral, to decorate

Put the ice cubes into a cocktail shaker. Pour the lemon juice, sugar syrup, and whiskey over the ice and shake until a frost forms. Pour, without straining, into a tumbler or Collins glass and add the orange slice and maraschino cherry impaled on a toothpick. Top up with soda water, stir lightly, and serve, decorated with an orange zest spiral.

Suburban

4–5 ice cubes
3 drops orange or Angostura bitters
3 measures bourbon or Scotch whiskey
1 measure port
1 measure dark rum

Put the ice cubes into a mixing glass. Shake the bitters over the ice and pour in the whiskey, port, and rum. Stir vigorously, then strain into a chilled cocktail glass.

Ritz Old-fashioned

lightly beaten egg white
superfine sugar
3 ice cubes, crushed
1$\frac{1}{2}$ measures bourbon whiskey
$\frac{1}{2}$ measure Grand Marnier
1 dash lemon juice
1 dash Angostura bitters
orange or lemon slice, to decorate
maraschino cherry, to decorate

Frost the rim of an old-fashioned glass by dipping it into the egg white,
then pressing it into the sugar. Put the crushed ice into a cocktail shaker
and add the bourbon, Grand Marnier, lemon juice, and bitters. Shake to
mix, then strain into a glass. Decorate with the orange or lemon slice and
a maraschino cherry.

New Yorker

2–3 ice cubes, cracked
1 measure Scotch whiskey
1 teaspoon fresh lime juice
1 teaspoon confectioner's sugar
finely grated zest of $\frac{1}{2}$ lemon
lemon zest spiral, to decorate

Put the cracked ice into a cocktail shaker and add the whiskey, lime juice,
and sugar. Shake until a frost forms. Strain into an old-fashioned glass.
Sprinkle the grated lemon zest over the surface and decorate the rim with
a lemon zest spiral.

Ritz Old-fashioned

New Yorker

Manhattan

4–5 ice cubes
1 measure sweet vermouth
3 measures rye or bourbon whiskey
maraschino cherry, to decorate (optional)

Put the ice cubes into a mixing glass. Pour the vermouth and whiskey over the ice. Stir vigorously, then strain into a chilled cocktail glass. Drop in a cherry, if you like.

Cassis

4–5 ice cubes
1 measure bourbon whiskey
½ measure dry vermouth
1 teaspoon crème de cassis
2 blueberries, to decorate

Put the ice cubes into a cocktail shaker and pour in the bourbon, vermouth, and crème de cassis. Shake well, then strain into a chilled cocktail glass and decorate with blueberries impaled on a toothpick.

Manhattan

Cassis

Mississippi Punch

crushed ice
3 drops Angostura bitters
1 teaspoon sugar syrup
juice of 1 lemon
1 measure brandy
1 measure dark rum
2 measures bourbon whiskey

Half-fill a tall glass with crushed ice. Shake the bitters over the ice. Pour in the sugar syrup and the lemon juice, then stir gently to mix thoroughly. Add the brandy, rum, and bourbon, in that order, stir once, and serve with straws.

Godfather Sour

ice cubes
1½ measures bourbon whiskey
1 measure Amaretto di Saronno liqueur
1 measure lemon juice
1 teaspoon sugar syrup
lemon slices, to decorate

Put some ice cubes into a cocktail shaker with the whiskey, Amaretto di Saronno, lemon juice and sugar syrup and shake well. Strain into a small old-fashioned glass filled with ice cubes and decorate with lemon slices.

Whiskey Sour

ice cubes
2 measures whiskey
1½ measures fresh lemon juice
1 egg white
2 tablespoons superfine sugar
4 dashes Angostura bitters
lemon slice, to decorate
maraschino cherry, to decorate

Put some ice cubes into a cocktail shaker with the whiskey, lemon juice, egg white, sugar, and bitters and shake well. Strain into a sour glass filled with ice cubes and decorate with a lemon slice and a maraschino cherry on a toothpick.

Bourbon Sloe Gin

ice cubes, and crushed ice
1½ measures bourbon whiskey
½ measure sloe gin
½ measure lemon juice
1 tablespoon sugar syrup
lemon and peach slices, to decorate

Put the ice cubes into a cocktail shaker with the bourbon and sloe gin and shake well. Strain into a cocktail glass over crushed ice. Decorate with lemon and peach slices.

I got rid of all those reporters.
What did you tell them?
We're out of Scotch.
What a gruesome idea.

NORA CHARLES (MYRNA LOY) & NICK CHARLES
(WILLIAM POWELL) – ANOTHER THIN MAN (1939)

Harlequin

5 white grapes, plus 2 to decorate
½ measure sweet vermouth
6 dashes orange bitters
crushed ice
2 measures Canadian Club whiskey

Muddle the white grapes, vermouth, and bitters in an old-fashioned glass. Half-fill the glass with crushed ice and stir well. Add the whiskey and top up with crushed ice. Decorate with the extra grapes.

Give me a whiskey, ginger ale on the side... and don't be stingy, baby.

ANNA (GRETA GARBO) – ANNA CHRISTIE (1930)

Skipper

4–5 ice cubes
4 drops grenadine
juice of ½ orange
1 measure dry vermouth
3 measures rye or Scotch whiskey
orange wedge, to decorate

Put the ice cubes into a mixing glass. Pour the grenadine over the ice and add the orange juice, vermouth, and whiskey. Stir vigorously until nearly frothy, then pour into a tumbler. Decorate with an orange wedge and serve with a straw.

Vanilla Daisy

crushed ice
2 measures bourbon whiskey
1 measure fresh lemon juice
1 measure vanilla syrup
1 teaspoon grenadine
2 maraschino cherries, to decorate

Put some crushed ice into a cocktail shaker with the bourbon, lemon juice, and vanilla syrup and shake well. Strain into an old-fashioned glass filled with crushed ice, then drizzle the grenadine through the drink. Decorate with maraschino cherries on a toothpick.

Whiskey Daisy

ice cubes
2 measures Scotch or bourbon whiskey
1 measure fresh lemon juice
1 teaspoon superfine sugar
1 teaspoon grenadine
soda water, to top up
lemon zest spiral, to decorate

Put some ice cubes into a cocktail shaker with the whiskey, lemon juice, sugar, and grenadine and shake well. Strain into an old-fashioned glass filled with ice cubes and top up with soda water, if you like. Decorate with a lemon zest spiral.

Vanilla Daisy

Whiskey Daisy

Sicilian Kiss

crushed ice
2 measures Southern Comfort
1 measure Amaretto di Saronno liqueur
lemon slice, to decorate

Put plenty of crushed ice into either a squat glass or old-fashioned glass
with the bourbon and Amaretto di Saronno and stir to mix. Decorate with a
lemon slice.

Irish Coffee

1 measure Irish whiskey
hot drip coffee
lightly whipped cream
ground coffee, to decorate

Put a bar spoon into a large wine glass, add the whiskey, then top up with hot coffee, and stir. Heat the cream very slightly and pour it into the bowl of the spoon on top of the coffee so that it float across the surface. Decorate with a pinch of ground coffee.

I never should have switched from Scotch to Martinis.

HUMPHREY BOGART'S LAST WORDS

WINE AND CHAMPAGNE

Cheshire Cat

4–5 ice cubes
1 measure brandy
1 measure sweet vermouth
1 measure fresh orange juice
Champagne, to top up
orange zest strip, to decorate
orange zest spiral, to decorate

Put the ice cubes into a mixing glass. Pour the brandy, vermouth, and orange juice over the ice and stir to mix. Strain into a Champagne flute and top up with Champagne. Squeeze the orange zest strip over the drink and decorate with an orange zest spiral.

Caribbean Champagne

1 tablespoon light rum
1 tablespoon crème de banane
1 dash Angostura bitters
Champagne, to top up
banana and pineapple slices, to decorate
maraschino cherry, to decorate

Pour the rum, crème de banane and bitters into a chilled Champagne flute. Top up with Champagne and stir gently. Decorate with the banana, pineapple, and maraschino cherry, all speared on a toothpick.

Caribbean Champagne

Man in the Moon

ice cubes
1 measure vodka
1/2 measure apricot brandy
1/2 measure lemon juice
2 dashes grenadine
chilled Champagne or sparkling wine, to top up

Put some ice cubes into a cocktail shaker with the vodka, apricot brandy, lemon juice, and grenadine and shake well. Strain into a Champagne glass and top up with chilled Champagne (or sparkling wine).

Black Velvet

4 measures Guinness
4 measures Champagne

Pour the Guinness into a large glass and carefully add the Champagne.

Black Velvet

Bellini

Frobisher

chopped ice
2 dashes Angostura bitters
3 tablespoons gin
chilled Champagne, to top up
lemon zest twist, to decorate

Fill a highball glass with chopped ice. Shake the bitters over the ice. Pour in the gin and top up with the chilled Champagne. Squeeze the lemon zest twist over the drink and drop it in.

Bellini

2 measures peach juice
4 measures chilled Champagne
1 dash grenadine (optional)
peach slice, to decorate (optional)

Mix the peach juice and chilled Champagne in a large Champagne saucer with a dash of grenadine, if using. Decorate with a peach slice, if you like.

Eve

several drops Pernod
1 tablespoon Cognac
2 teaspoons sugar
2 teaspoons Curaçao
pink Champagne, to top up

Add the Pernod drops to a Champagne saucer; swirl gently to coat the inside of the glass. Pour in the Cognac. Soak the sugar in the Curaçao until it has dissolved, then add them to the Cognac and stir gently. Top up the glass with pink Champagne.

Aria Classic

1 brown sugar cube
3 dashes Angostura bitters
1 measure Grand Marnier
Champagne, to top up
orange zest twist, to decorate

Drop the sugar cube into a chilled Champagne flute and shake the Angostura bitters over it. Add the Grand Marnier and stir briefly. Top up with Champagne and decorate with an orange zest twist.

Aria Classic

Carlton

ice cubes
3 measures orange juice
2 tablespoons Grand Marnier
1 egg white
2–3 dashes peach bitters
Champagne, to top up
maraschino cherries, to decorate

Put some ice cubes into a cocktail shaker and pour the Grand Marnier, egg white and bitters over them. Shake very well. Strain into a Champagne saucer, top up with Champagne, and stir gently. Decorate with maraschino cherries.

Champagne Cooler

crushed ice
1 measure brandy
1 measure Cointreau
Champagne, to top up
mint sprigs, to decorate

Put some crushed ice into a Champagne sucer. Pour the brandy and Cointreau over the ice. Top up with Champagne and stir. Decorate with mint sprigs.

California Dreaming

ice cubes
2 dashes kirsch
3 measures pineapple juice
1 dash lemon juice
chilled Champagne, to top up
pineapple wedge, to decorate

Put some ice cubes into a food processor or blender with the kirsch and fruit juices and blend for 30 seconds. Pour into a wine glass and top up with chilled Champagne. Decorate with a pineapple wedge.

Loving Cup

8 sugar cubes
2 lemons
1/2 bottle medium or sweet sherry
1/4 bottle brandy
1 bottle dry sparkling white wine

Rub the sugar cubes over the lemons to absorb the zest's oils. Thinly peel the lemons and remove as much of the pith as possible. Thinly slice the lemons and set aside. Put the lemon zest, sherry, brandy, and sugar cubes into a pitcher and stir until the sugar has dissolved. Cover and chill for about 30 minutes. To serve, add the wine to the pitcher and float the lemon slices on top. Serves 12

Loving Cup

Head-over-heels

Cool Shower

ice cubes
zest of 1 orange
3 measures sparkling dry white wine
1 measure Campari
2 measures orange juice

Put some ice cubes into a wine goblet with the orange zest. Add the sparkling wine, Campari, and orange juice.

Head-over-heels

4–5 ice cubes
juice of 1 lime
3 measures vodka
sugar cube
3 drops Angostura bitters
Champagne, to top up

Put the ice cubes into a cocktail shaker. Pour the lime juice and vodka over the ice and shake until a frost forms. Drop a sugar cube into a glass and shake the bitters over it. Strain the contents of the shaker into the glass and top up with Champagne.

Lush Crush

2 strawberries, hulled
1 dash sugar syrup
2 lime wedges
1 measure Absolut Kurant vodka
ice cubes
Champagne, to top up
strawberry slices, to decorate

Muddle the strawberries, sugar syrup and lime wedges into a cocktail shaker. Add the vodka and some ice cubes. Shake and double strain into a chilled Champagne flute. Top up with Champagne, and decorate with a strawberry slice.

Celebration Cocktail

1 lemon wedge
superfine sugar
ice cubes
1 measure brandy
1 dash Bénédictine
1 dash crème de mure
chilled Champagne, to top up

Frost the rim of a Champagne flute by moistening it with the lemon wedge then pressing it into the sugar. Put some ice cubes into a cocktail shaker and add the brandy, Bénédictine, and crème de mure. Shake well, strain into the prepared glass, and top up with Champagne.

Celebration Cocktail

Buck's Twizz

1 measure chilled orange juice
1/2 measure Maraschino liqueur
1 measure Absolut Mandarin vodka
chilled Champagne, to top up
rindless pink grapefruit slice, to decorate

Pour the orange juice and Maraschino liqueur into a chilled Champagne saucer, then add the vodka and Champagne together (this prevents excessive fizzing). Float a rindless pink grapefruit slice on the surface.

Buck's Fizz

2 measures chilled orange juice
6 measures chilled Champagne

Pour the chilled orange juice into a Champagne flute or cocktail glass and add the chilled Champagne.

Buck's Twizz

Buck's Fizz

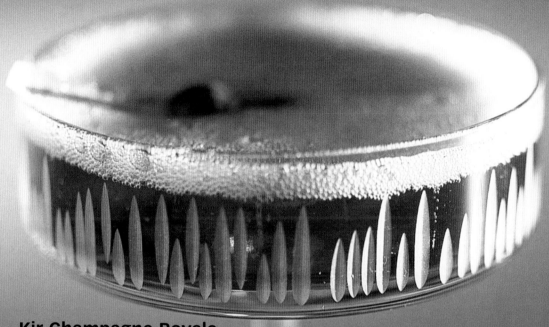

Kir Champagne Royale

Kir Champagne Royale

1 teaspoon vodka
2 teaspoons crème de cassis
Champagne, to top up

Put the vodka and crème de cassis into a Champagne saucer. Top up with Champagne.

Cavendish

chopped ice
2 drops Angostura bitters
2 measures vodka
chilled Champagne, to top up
lemon zest twist, to decorate

Fill a highball glass with chopped ice. Shake the bitters over the ice. Pour in the vodka and top up with chilled Champagne. Squeeze the lemon zest twist over the drink and drop it in.

Lime Fizz

1 lime wedge
1 measure lime vodka
1 measure orange juice
ice cubes
Champagne, to top up
Lime zest twists, to decorate

Squeeze the lime wedge into a cocktail shaker and add the vodka and orange juice with some ice cubes. Shake very briefly and double strain into a chilled Champagne flute. Top up with Champagne and decorate with lime zest twists.

Pernod Fizz

1 measure Pernod
6 measures chilled Champagne
lime slice, to decorate

Put the Pernod into a Champagne flute and swirl it round to coat the inside of the glass. Slowly pour in the chilled Champagne, allowing the drink to become cloudy. Decorate with a lime slice.

An Irishman is never drunk as long as he can hold onto one blade of grass and not fall off the face of the earth. OLD IRISH TOAST

Gorgeous Grace

ice cubes
1 measure brandy
1/2 measure Cointreau
chilled Champagne, or sparkling dry white wine, to top up
orange slice, to decorate

Put some ice cubes into a mixing glass with the brandy and Cointreau and mix gently. Pour into a Champagne glass and top up with chilled Champagne or sparkling wine. Decorate with an orange slice.

Bubble Berry

2 raspberries
2 blackberries, plus extra to decorate
1/2 measure framboise liqueur
1/2 measure crème de mure
3 measures Champagne

Muddle the raspberries and blackberries in a Champagne flute. Add the framboise and the crème de mure. Top up with the Champagne. Decorate the glass with a blackberry and serve immediately.

Bubble Berry

Bombay Punch

ice cubes
5 cups brandy
5 cups sherry
2/3 cups Maraschino liqueur
2/3 cups orange Curaçao
5 quarts chilled Champagne
2½ quarts sparkling mineral water
fruit in season, to decorate
mint sprigs, to decorate

Put plenty of ice cubes into a large punch bowl with all the other ingredients and stir gently. Decorate with fruit and mint sprigs. Keep the punch bowl packed with ice. Serves 25–30

Drunk is feeling sophisticated when you can't say it. UNKNOWN

Paddy's Night

3 ice cubes, cracked
1 measure green crème de menthe
1 measure Irish whiskey
Champagne, to top up

Put the cracked ice into a cocktail shaker with the crème de menthe and
whiskey and shake well. Strain into a large wine glass and top up with
Champagne.

Chablis Cup

3 ripe peaches, skinned, pitted, and sliced
1 orange, thinly sliced
maraschino cherries
3 teaspoons superfine sugar
1 bottle Chablis
4 measures Grand Marnier
4 measures Kirsch

Put the fruit and sugar in a punch bowl. Pour in the Chablis, Grand Marnier, and kirsch and stir. Cover and chill for 1 hour. Serves 15–20

Mango Bellini

3 measures mango juice
pink Champagne, to top up

Pour the mango juice into a Champagne flute and top up with pink
Champagne. Stir gently to mix and serve immediately.

La Seine Fizz

1 measure Cognac
1/2 measure Fraise de Bois
1/2 measure lemon juice
1 dash orange bitters
2 strawberries, hulled and chopped
sugar syrup, to taste
3 measures Champagne
1/2 measure Grand Marnier
strawberry wedge and mint sprig, to decorate

Put the Cognac, Fraise de Bois, lemon juice, bitters, and strawberries
into a cocktail shaker with sugar syrup to taste. Shake and strain into
a Champagne glass. Top up with the Champagne and pour the Grand
Marnier over the top. Decorate with a strawberry wedge and a mint sprig.

Grand Mimosa

1 measure Grand Marnier
2 measures orange juice, chilled
chilled Champagne, to top up

Pour the Grand Marnier and orange juice into a Champagne flute and top up with chilled Champagne.

Grandaddy Mimosa

ice cubes
1 measure Havana Club 3-year-old rum
1 measure orange juice
1/2 measure fresh lemon juice
chilled Champagne, to top up
orange zest twist, to decorate
1 dash grenadine

Put some ice cubes into a shaker with the rum and fruit juices and shake to mix. Strain into a large Champagne flute, then top up with chilled Champagne. Drop in the grenadine and decorate with an orange zest twist.

Grand Mimosa

Grandaddy Mimosa

Martini Royale

2$\frac{1}{2}$ measures ice-cold vodka
$\frac{1}{4}$ measure crème de cassis
Champagne, to top up
lemon zest twist, to decorate

Pour the vodka into a chilled Martini glass, then stir in the cassis. Top up with Champagne, then add a lemon zest twist.

ChamPino

ice cubes
1 measure Campari
1¼ measures sweet vermouth
Champagne, to top up
lemon zest twist, to decorate

Put some ice cubes into a cocktail shaker with the Campari and vermouth
and shake well. Strain into a chilled Martini glass. Top up with chilled
Champagne and decorate with a lemon zest twist.

Ritz Fizz I

1 dash blue Curaçao
1 dash lemon juice
1 dash Amaretto di Saronno liqueur
Champagne, to top up
lemon zest spiral, to decorate

Pour the Curaçao, lemon juice, and Amaretto di Saronno into a glass and top up with Champagne. Stir gently to mix and decorate the drink with a lemon zest spiral.

Ritz Fizz II

ice cubes
1/2 measure crème de cassis
1/2 measure Poire William liqueur
chilled Champagne, to top up
pear slices, peeled, to decorate

Put some ice cubes into a mixing glass with the crème de cassis and Poire William liqueur and stir to mix well. Strain into a Champagne flute and top up with chilled Champagne. Decorate with peeled pear slices.

Ritz Fizz II

Ritz Fizz I

Champagne Julep

2 mint sprigs
1 tablespoon sugar syrup
crushed ice
1 measure brandy
Champagne, to top up

Muddle the mint with the sugar syrup in a large wine glass. Fill the glass with crushed ice, then add the brandy. Top up with Champagne and stir gently.

An intelligent man is sometimes forced to be drunk to spend time with his fools.

FOR WHOM THE BELL TOLLS, ERNEST HEMINGWAY

Slinky Mink

$1/2$ measure raspberry purée
1 dash sugar syrup
2 teaspoons lime juice
Champagne, to top up
lime zest twist, to decorate

Pour the raspberry purée, sugar syrup and lime juice into the bottom of a chilled Champagne flute. Top up with Champagne, stir lightly, and decorate with a lime zest twist.

Always remember that I have taken more out of alcohol then alcohol has taken out of me. WINSTON CHURCHILL

Champagne Romanov Fizz

2 ice cubes
8–10 ripe strawberries, hulled
4 measures orange juice
4 measures Champagne
strawberry slice, to decorate
mint sprig, to decorate

Put 1 ice cube into a blender or food processor with the strawberries and
orange juice and blend until smooth. Put the other ice cube into a tall glass
and add the strawberry liquid. Top up with the Champagne. Stir briskly
and serve immediately.

*There can't be good living where
there is not good drinking.*

BENJAMIN FRANKLIN

Classic Champagne Cocktail

1 sugar cube
1–2 dashes Angostura bitters
1 measure brandy
chilled Champagne, to top up
orange slice, to decorate

Saturate the sugar cube with the bitters, then drop it into a chilled cocktail or Champagne flute. Add the brandy, then top up with chilled Champagne. Decorate with an orange slice.

The Classic's Classic

1 sugar cube
2 dashes Angostura bitters
1 measure Grand Marnier
4 measures chilled Champagne
orange zest, to decorate

Saturate the sugar cube with the bitters, then drop it into a Champagne flute. Add the Grand Marnier, then top up with the chilled Champagne. Drop the orange zest in the drink to decorate.

**Classic
Champagne
Cocktail**

**The
Classic's
Classic**

Russian Spring Punch

ice cubes
1/2 measure crème de cassis
1 measure fresh lemon juice
2 tablespoons sugar syrup
chilled Champagne, to top up
2 measures Absolut vodka
lemon slice, to decorate
berries, to decorate

Fill a sling glass with ice cubes. Pour over the crème de cassis, lemon juice, and sugar syrup. Add the Champagne and vodka at the same time (this prevents excessive fizzing) and stir. Decorate with a lemon slice and berries.

Parisian Spring Punch

ice cubes, plus crushed ice, to serve
1 1/2 measures Calvados
1/2 measure fresh lemon juice
1/2 measure Noilly Prat vermouth
1 teaspoon superfine sugar
chilled Champagne, to top up
apple slices, to decorate

Put some ice cubes into a cocktail shaker with the Calvados, lemon juice, vermouth, and sugar and shake to mix. Strain over crushed ice in a sling glass and top up with chilled Champagne. Decorate with apple slices.

Russian Spring Punch

Parisian
Spring
Punch

TEQUILA

Mexicana

8–10 ice cubes
1¼ measures tequila
¾ measure framboise liqueur
¾ measure fresh lemon juice
3½ measures pineapple juice
pineapple wedge, to decorate
lemon slice, to decorate

Put half of the ice cubes into a cocktail shaker with the tequila, framboise, and fruit juices and shake vigorously for about 10 seconds. Pour the drink over the remaining ice cubes in a large highball glass and decorate with a pineapple wedge and a lemon slice.

Maracuja

1 fresh ripe passion fruit
4–5 ice cubes
1¼ measures gold tequila
1 tablespoon Creole Shrub
¾ measure fresh lime juice
2 teaspoons Cointreau
1 teaspoon passion fruit syrup
Cape gooseberry, to decorate

Cut the passion fruit in half and scoop the flesh into a cocktail shaker. Add the ice cubes, tequila, Creole Shrub, lime juice, Cointreau and passion fruit syrup and shake vigorously for 10 seconds. Strain through a fine sieve into a chilled cocktail glass. Decorate with a Cape gooseberry.

Maracuja

Forest Fruit

1 lime wedge
light brown sugar
2 blackberries, plus extra to decorate
2 raspberries, plus extra to decorate
2 teaspoons Chambord raspberry liqueur
2 teaspoons crème de mure
1¼ measures tequila
2 teaspoons Cointreau
1¼ measures fresh lemon juice
crushed ice
lemon slices, to decorate

Frost the rim of an old-fashioned glass by moistening it with the lime wedge and pressing it into the brown sugar. Drop the blackberries and raspberries into the glass and muddle to a pulp. Stir in the Chambord and crème de mure. Pour in the tequila, Cointreau, and lemon juice, fill with crushed ice, and stir gently, lifting the muddled berries from the bottom of the glass. Decorate with lemon slices, a blackberry, and a raspberry.

Border Crossing

ice cubes
1½ measures gold tequila
1 measure fresh lime juice
1 measure clear honey
4 dashes orange bitters
3 measures dry ginger ale
blueberries, to decorate
lime wedges, to decorate

Put some ice cubes into a cocktail shaker with the tequila, lime juice, honey, and bitters and shake well. Pour into a highball glass and top up with the dry ginger ale. Decorate with blueberries and lime wedges.

Forest Fruit

Cobalt Margarita

Baja Sour

4–5 ice cubes
1¼ measures gold tequila
2 teaspoons sugar syrup
1¼ measures fresh lemon juice
2 dashes orange bitters
½ egg white
1 tablespoon Amontillado sherry
lemon slices, to decorate
orange rind spiral, to decorate

Put the ice cubes into a cocktail shaker with the tequila, sugar syrup, lemon juice, bitters, and egg white and shake vigorously. Pour into a large sour glass and drizzle the sherry over the drink. Decorate with lemon slices and an orange rind spiral.

Cobalt Margarita

1 lime wedge
fine sea salt
4–5 ice cubes
1¼ measures tequila
2 teaspoons Cointreau
½ measure blue Curaçao
¾ measure fresh lime juice
¾ measure fresh grapefruit juice
lime rind spiral, to decorate

Frost the rim of a chilled cocktail glass by moistening it with a lime wedge then pressing it into salt. Put the ice cubes into a cocktail shaker with the tequila, Cointreau, blue Curaçao, and fruit juices and shake vigorously for 10 seconds. Strain into the prepared glass. Decorate with a lime rind spiral.

Sunburn

ice cubes
3/4 measure gold tequila
1 tablespoon Cointreau
6 measures cranberry juice
orange slice, to decorate

Fill a large highball glass with ice cubes and pour in the tequila, Cointreau, and cranberry juice. Decorate with an orange slice.

Sombrero

4–5 ice cubes
3/4 measure gold tequila
3/4 measure white crème de cacao
3 1/2 measures light cream
grated nutmeg, to decorate

Put the ice cubes into a cocktail shaker. Pour in the tequila, crème de cacao, and cream and shake vigorously for 10 seconds. Strain into a chilled Margarita glass. Sprinkle with grated nutmeg.

Sombrero

Tequila de Coco

crushed ice
1 measure tequila
1 measure fresh lemon juice
1 measure coconut syrup
3 dashes Maraschino liqueur
lemon slice, to decorate

Put some crushed ice into a blender and add the tequila, lemon juice, coconut syrup, and Maraschino liqueur. Blend for a few seconds, then pour into a Collins glass and decorate with a lemon slice.

Tequini

ice cubes
3 dashes orange bitters
3 measures tequila blanco
2 teaspoons dry French vermouth, preferably Noilly Prat
black olive, to decorate

Fill a mixing glass with ice cubes, then add the bitters and tequila. Stir gently for 10 seconds. Put the vermouth into a chilled cocktail glass and swirl to coat the inside, then tip it out. Stir the bitters and tequila for a further 10 seconds and strain into the cocktail glass. Decorate with a black olive.

Tequini

Mexican Mule

1 lime
1 dash sugar syrup
crushed ice
1 measure José Cuervo Gold tequila
1 measure Kahlúa
dry ginger ale, to top up

Cut the lime into slices, put them into a highball glass and muddle with the sugar syrup. Half-fill the glass with crushed ice and add the tequila and Kahlúa. Stir well, then top up with dry ginger ale.

Pink Cadillac Convertible

3 lime wedges
fine sea salt
ice cubes
1¼ measures gold tequila
½ measure cranberry juice
¾ measure Grand Marnier
lime wedge, to decorate

Frost the rim of a large old-fashioned glass by moistening with a lime wedge, then pressing it into the salt. Fill the glass with ice cubes. Pour the tequila and cranberry juice into a cocktail shaker. Squeeze the juice from the remaining lime wedges into the shaker, pressing the rind to release its oils, then drop the wedges in. Add 4–5 ice cubes and shake vigorously for 10 seconds, then strain into the glass. Drizzle the Grand Marnier over the top and decorate with lime wedges.

Pink Cadillac Convertible

Thigh High

3 strawberries, hulled
1 teaspoon strawberry syrup
4–5 ice cubes
1 measure tequila
1 measure dark crème de cacao
1½ measures light cream
1 strawberry dipped in cocoa, to decorate

Muddle the strawberries and strawberry syrup in a cocktail shaker. Add the
ice cubes with the tequila, crème de cacao and cream and shake to mix.
Strain into a large, chilled cocktail glass and decorate with a strawberry
dipped in cocoa.

Brooklyn Bomber

5 ice cubes, crushed
1 measure tequila
½ measure Cointreau
½ measure cherry brandy
½ measure Galliano
1 measure lemon juice
orange slice, to decorate
maraschino cherry, to decorate

Put half of the crushed ice into a cocktail shaker and add the tequila, Cointreau, cherry brandy, Galliano, and lemon juice. Shake to mix and pour it over the remaining ice in a hurricane glass. Decorate with an orange slice and a maraschino cherry and serve with straws.

The first drink with water, the second without water, the third like water.

SPANISH MAXIM

Jalisco Swizzle

4–5 ice cubes, plus crushed ice to serve
3 dashes Angostura bitters
3/4 measure gold tequila
3/4 measure golden rum
1 1/4 measures fresh lime juice
3/4 measure passion fruit juice
2 teaspoons sugar syrup
soda water, to top up
lime slice, to decorate
mint sprig, to decorate

Put the ice cubes into a cocktail shaker with the bitters, tequila, rum, fruit juices, and sugar syrup and shake vigorously. Strain into a highball glass filled with crushed ice. Top up with soda and stir briefly until a frost forms. Decorate with a lime slice and a mint sprig.

Sour Apple

4–5 ice cubes
1 1/4 measures tequila
2 teaspoons Cointreau
1 tablespoon apple schnapps
3/4 measure fresh lime juice
3/4 measure unsweetened apple juice
Granny Smith apple wedge, to decorate

Put the ice cubes into a cocktail shaker with the tequila, Cointreau, schnapps, and fruit juices and shake vigorously for 10 seconds. Strain into a chilled cocktail glass. Decorate with an apple wedge.

Sour Apple

Viva Maria

ice cubes, plus crushed ice to serve
1 measure tequila
1/2 measure fresh lime juice
1/4 measure Maraschino liqueur
1/2 teaspoon grenadine
1/2 egg white
lemon and lime slices, to decorate
maraschino cherry, to decorate

Put the ice cubes into a cocktail shaker and pour the tequila, lime juice, Maraschino liqueur, grenadine, and egg white over them. Shake well and strain into a Champagne saucer filled with crushed ice. Decorate with lemon and lime slices and a maraschino cherry.

Margarita

1 lime wedge
rock salt
ice cubes
2 measures Herrudura Reposado tequila
1 measure lime juice
1 measure Triple Sec
lime slice, to decorate

Frost the rim of a Margarita glass by moistening it with a lime wedge, then pressing it into the salt. Put some ice cubes into a cocktail shaker with the tequila, lime juice, and Triple Sec. Shake well. Strain into the prepared glass. Decorate with a lime slice.

Margarita

Ruby Rita

Mexicola

4 lime wedges
crushed ice
1¼ measures tequila
6 measures cola

Muddle the lime wedges in a large highball glass. Fill the glass with crushed ice, then pour in the tequila and cola. Stir gently, lifting the lime wedges through the drink.

Ruby Rita

1¼ measures fresh pink grapefruit juice
fine sea salt
ice cubes
1¼ measures gold tequila
¾ measure Cointreau
pink grapefruit wedge, to decorate

Frost the rim of an old-fashioned glass by moistening it with some of the pink grapefruit juice and pressing it into the salt. Fill the glass with ice cubes. Pour the tequila, Cointreau, and the remaining pink grapefruit juice into a cocktail shaker, fill it with more ice and shake vigorously. Strain into the prepared glass and decorate with a pink grapefruit wedge.

Dirty Sanchez

ice cubes
2 teaspoons Noilly Prat vermouth
2 measures gold tequila (preferably Anejo)
2 teaspoons brine from a jar of black olives
2 black olives, to decorate

Fill a mixing glass with ice cubes and add the vermouth. Stir to coat the
ice, then discard the excess vermouth. Add the tequila and brine and stir
until thoroughly chilled. Strain into a chilled cocktail glass and decorate
with black olives on a toothpick.

Frostbite

4–5 ice cubes
1 measure tequila
1 measure heavy cream
1 measure white crème de cacao
½ measure white crème de menthe
hot cocoa mix, to decorate

Put the ice cubes into a cocktail shaker. Pour in the tequila, cream, crème de cacao, and crème de menthe and shake vigorously for 10 seconds. Strain into a chilled cocktail glass. Sprinkle with hot cocoa mix.

Texas Tea

ice cubes
¾ measure tequila
1 tablespoon white rum
1 tablespoon Cointreau
2 teaspoons sugar syrup
¾ measure fresh lemon juice
¾ measure fresh orange juice
3½ measures strong fruit tea, chilled
orange and lemon slices, to decorate
mint sprig, to decorate

Put a handful of ice cubes into a
cocktail shaker with the tequila, rum,
Cointreau, sugar syrup, fruit juices,
and tea and shake vigorously. Strain
into a sling glass filled with fresh ice
cubes. Decorate with orange and
lemon slices and a mint sprig.

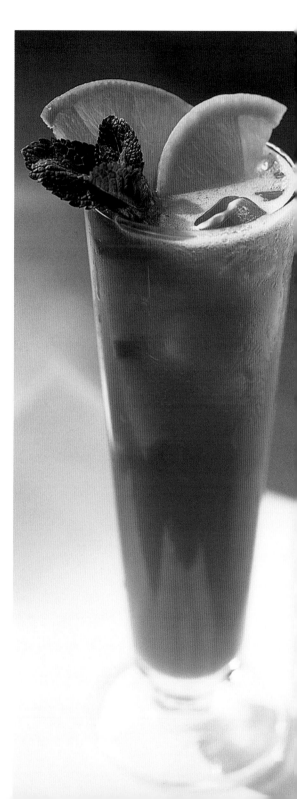

' Look, sweetheart, I can
drink you under any
goddamn table you want, so
don't worry about me. '

MARTHA (ELIZABETH TAYLOR) – WHO'S
AFRAID OF VIRGINIA WOOLF? (1966)

Grand Margarita

1 lime wedge, plus 1 to decorate
rock salt
ice cubes
1½ measures silver tequila
1 measure Grand Marnier
1 measure lime juice

Frost the rim of a Margarita glass by moistening it with the lime wedge then pressing it into the salt. Put some ice cubes into a cocktail shaker with the tequila, Grand Marnier, and lime juice and shake well. Double strain into the prepared glass and decorate with a lime wedge.

Rude Cosmopolitan

ice cubes
1½ measures gold tequila
1 measure Cointreau
1 measure cranberry juice
½ measure fresh lime juice
flamed orange rind twist, to decorate (see page 539)

Put some ice cubes into a cocktail shaker, add the tequila, Cointreau, and fruit juices and shake well. Strain into a chilled Martini glass and decorate with a flamed orange rind twist.

South of the Border

4–5 ice cubes
1¼ measures tequila
¾ measure Kahlúa
1¼ measures fresh lime juice

Put the ice cubes into a cocktail shaker with the tequila, Kahlúa, and lime juice and shake vigorously for 10 seconds. Strain the drink into a chilled cocktail glass.

South of the Border

Desert Daisy

crushed ice
1 measure tequila
1¼ measures fresh lime juice
2 teaspoons sugar syrup
1 tablespoon Fraise de Bois
blackberry and strawberry, to decorate
lime and orange wedges, to decorate
mint sprig, to decorate

Half-fill a large old-fashioned glass with crushed ice. Pour in the tequila, lime juice, and sugar syrup and stir gently until a frost forms. Add more crushed ice then float the Fraise de Bois on top. Decorate with a blackberry, a strawberry, a lime wedge, an orange wedge, and a mint sprig.

Playa Del Mar

ice cubes
1 orange slice
light brown sugar and sea salt, mixed
1¼ measures gold tequila
¾ measure Grand Marnier
2 teaspoons fresh lime juice
¾ measure cranberry juice
¾ measure pineapple juice
pineapple wedge, to decorate
orange rind spiral, to decorate

Frost the rim of a sling glass by moistening it with the orange slice, then pressing it into the sugar and salt mixture. Fill the glass with ice cubes. Pour the tequila, Grand Marnier, and fruit juices into a cocktail shaker. Fill the shaker with ice cubes and shake vigorously for 10 seconds, then strain into the sling glass. Decorate with a pineapple wedge and orange rind spiral.

Playa Del Mar

Silk Stocking

hot cocoa mix
4–5 ice cubes
¾ measure tequila
¾ measure white crème de cacao
3½ measures light cream
2 teaspoons grenadine

Frost the rim of a chilled cocktail glass by dipping it into water, then pressing it into the hot cocoa mix. Put the ice cubes into a cocktail shaker with the tequila, crème de cacao, cream, and grenadine. Shake vigorously for 10 seconds, then strain into the prepared glass.

Pale Original

ice cubes
2 measures gold tequila
½ measure ginger syrup
½ measure fresh lime juice
1 measure guava juice
lime wedges, to decorate

Put some ice cubes into a cocktail shaker with the tequila, ginger syrup and fruit juices and shake well. Strain into a chilled cocktail glass.

Raspberry Beret

½ measure light crème de cacao
1 measure chilled gold tequila
1 plump raspberry

Pour the crème de cacao into a shot glass. Using the back of a bar spoon, slowly float the tequila over the crème de cacao. Slowly lower the raspberry into the drink – it will settle between the 2 spirits.

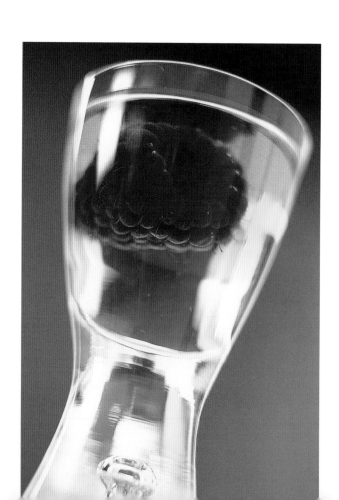

El Diablo

ice cubes
1¼ measures tequila gold
¾ measure lime juice
2 teaspoons grenadine
3½ measures dry ginger ale
lime slice, to decorate

Fill a large highball glass with ice cubes and pour in the tequila, lime juice, and grenadine. Top up with dry ginger ale and stir gently. Decorate with a lime slice.

Beckoning Lady

6–8 ice cubes
2 measures tequila
4 measures passion fruit juice
1–2 teaspoons Galliano
maraschino cherries, to decorate

Fill a hurricane or highball glass with the ice. Using the back of a bar
spoon, slowly add the tequila and passion fruit juice and stir well to mix.
Float the Galliano on top in a layer about a half-inch deep and decorate
with maraschino cherries.

Batanga

1 Mexican lime
rock salt
ice cubes
2 measures Tequileno Blanco tequila
Mexican cola, to top up

Cut the tip off the lime and make a slit in its side. Dip in the salt and run it
around the edge of an old-fashioned glass. Fill the glass with ice cubes and
add the tequila. Squeeze half of the lime juice into the drink, then stir it
with the knife used to cut the lime while topping it up with Mexican cola.

Batanga

Tijuana Sling

Tijuana Sling

ice cubes
1¼ measures tequila
¾ measure crème de cassis
¾ measure fresh lime juice
2 dashes Peychaud bitters
3½ measures dry ginger ale
lime slice, to decorate
blackcurrants or blueberries, to decorate

Put some ice cubes into a cocktail shaker with the tequila, crème de cassis, lime juice, and bitters and shake vigorously. Pour into a large sling glass, then top up with dry ginger ale. Decorate with a lime slice and some blackcurrants or blueberries.

Cadillac

3 lime wedges
fine sea salt
1¼ measures gold tequila
½ measure Cointreau
1¼ measures fresh lime juice
4–5 ice cubes
2 teaspoons Grand Marnier
lime slice, to decorate

Frost the rim of a chilled cocktail glass by moistening it with a lime wedge, then pressing it into the salt. Pour the tequila, Cointreau, and lime juice into a cocktail shaker. Squeeze the juice from the remaining lime wedges into the shaker, pressing the rind to release its oils, and drop the wedges in. Add the ice cubes and shake vigorously for 10 seconds, then strain into the prepared glass. Drizzle the Grand Marnier over the top and decorate with a lime slice.

Mexican Bulldog

ice cubes
¾ measure tequila
¾ measure Kahlúa
1¼ measures light cream
3½ measures cola
hot cocoa mix, to decorate

Put some ice cubes into a highball glass. Pour in the tequila, Kahlúa, and cream, then top up with the cola. Stir gently and serve decorated with hot cocoa mix.

Pancho Villa

4–5 ice cubes
1 measure tequila
½ measure Tia Maria
1 teaspoon Cointreau

Put the ice cubes into a cocktail shaker and pour in the tequila, Tia Maria, and Cointreau. Shake until a frost forms, then strain into a chilled cocktail glass.

Brave Bull

ice cubes
$^3/_4$ measure tequila
$^3/_4$ measure Kahlúa

Fill an old-fashioned glass with ice cubes. Pour in the tequila and Kahlúa and stir gently.

Passion Fruit Margarita

lime wedge
coarse sea salt
ice cubes
$1^1/_2$ measures gold tequila
1 measure Cointreau
1 teaspoon passion fruit syrup
1 measure fresh lime juice
pulp and seeds of 1 passion fruit
lime wedges, to decorate

Frost the rim of a Margarita glass by moistening it with a lime wedge and pressing it into the salt. Put some ice cubes into a cocktail shaker with the tequila, Cointreau, passion fruit syrup, lime juice, and half of the passion fruit pulp and shake well. Double strain into the prepared glass. Add the remaining passion fruit pulp and decorate with lime wedges.

Acapulco Bliss

4–5 ice cubes
¾ measure tequila
1 tablespoon Pisang Ambon (banana liqueur)
2 teaspoons Galliano
¾ measure fresh lemon juice
3½ measures passion fruit juice
¾ measure light cream
lemon slices, to decorate
pineapple wedge, to decorate
mint sprig, to decorate

Put the ice cubes into a cocktail shaker with the tequila, Pisang Ambon, Galliano, fruit juices, and cream and shake vigorously. Pour into a large sling glass and decorate with lemon slices, a pineapple wedge, and a mint sprig.

Tequila Slammer

1 measure gold tequila
1 measure Champagne

Pour the tequila into a shot glass. Slowly top it up with Champagne. Cover the top of the glass with the palm of your hand to seal the contents inside and grip it with your fingers. Briskly pick up the glass and slam it down on to a surface to make the drink fizz, then quickly gulp it down in one, while it is still fizzing.

Sometimes too much to drink is barely enough.

MARK TWAIN

Agave
Julep

Agave Julep

8 torn mint leaves
1 tablespoon sugar syrup
1¼ measures gold tequila
1¼ measures fresh lime juice
crushed ice
lime wedge, to decorate
mint sprig, to decorate

Muddle the mint leaves with the sugar syrup in a highball glass. Add the tequila and lime juice, fill the glass with crushed ice, and stir vigorously to mix. Decorate with a lime wedge and a mint sprig.

Rosarita Bay Breeze

ice cubes
1¼ measures tequila
6 measures cranberry juice
1½ measures pineapple juice
orange slice, to decorate

Put some ice cubes into a large highball glass and pour in the tequila and cranberry juice. Float the pineapple juice over the top of the drink and decorate it with an orange slice.

South for the Summer

Tequila Sunrise

Tequila Sunrise

ice cubes
2 measures tequila
4 measures orange juice
2 teaspoons grenadine
orange slices, to decorate

Put some ice cubes into a cocktail shaker with the tequila and orange juice and shake to mix. Strain into a highball glass filled with ice cubes. Slowly pour in the grenadine and allow it to settle. Decorate with an orange slice.

South for the Summer

2 teaspoons grenadine
crushed ice
2 measures tequila
3 measures orange juice
4 pineapple chunks
pineapple leaf, to decorate
orange rind, to decorate

Spoon the grenadine into a highball glass. Put some crushed ice into a food processor or blender with the tequila, orange juice, and pineapple chunks and blend until slushy. Pour the mixture over the grenadine, decorate with a pineapple leaf and an orange twist and stir just before serving.

Rooster Booster

ice cubes
1¼ measures tequila
6 measures fresh grapefruit juice
1 tablespoon grenadine
3½ measures soda water
lime slice, to decorate
maraschino cherry, to decorate

Put some ice cubes into a large highball glass. Pour in the tequila, grapefruit juice, and grenadine, stir gently, then top up with soda water. Decorate with a lime slice and a maraschino cherry.

Mockingbird

ice cubes
1¼ measures tequila
¾ measure green crème de menthe
1¼ measures fresh lime juice
lemon rind spiral, to decorate

Put some ice cubes into a cocktail shaker with the tequila, crème de menthe, and lime juice and shake vigorously for about 10 seconds. Strain into a chilled cocktail glass. Decorate with a lemon rind spiral.

Mockingbird

Alleluia

ice cubes
¾ measure tequila
½ measure blue Curaçao
2 teaspoons Maraschino syrup
1 dash egg white
¾ measure fresh lemon juice
3½ measures bitter lemon
lemon slice, to decorate
maraschino cherry, to decorate
mint sprig, to decorate

Put 4–5 ice cubes into a cocktail shaker with the tequila, Curaçao, Maraschino syrup, egg white and lemon juice and shake vigorously. Strain into a large highball glass filled with ice cubes. Top up with the bitter lemon and stir gently. Decorate with a lemon slice, a maraschino cherry and a mint sprig.

Honey Water

4–5 ice cubes
1¼ measures gold tequila
¾ measure sweet vermouth
3 dashes Angostura bitters
3 dashes Peychaud bitters
2 teaspoons Grand Marnier
maraschino cherry, to decorate
orange rind spiral, to decorate

Put the ice cubes into a mixing glass, pour in the tequila, vermouth, and bitters and stir gently for 10 seconds. Put the Grand Marnier into a chilled cocktail glass, swirl it round to coat the inside of the glass, then tip it out. Stir the contents of the mixing glass again for 10 seconds then strain into the cocktail glass. Decorate with a maraschino cherry and an orange rind spiral.

Honey Water

OTHER SPIRITS AND LIQUEURS

Slippery Nipple

1 measure Sambuca
1/2 measure Baileys Irish Cream

Pour the Sambuca into a shot glass. Using the back of a bar spoon, slowly float the Baileys over the Sambuca.

Go West

ice cubes
1/2 measure Frangelico hazelnut liqueur
1 measure Limoncello lemon liqueur
1 measure dry white wine
1/2 measure sugar syrup
1/2 measure lemon juice
lemon zest twist, to decorate

Put some ice cubes into a cocktail shaker with the Frangelico, Limoncello, wine, sugar syrup, and juice and shake well. Double strain into a chilled Martini glass. Decorate with a lemon zest twist.

Go West

Strawberry Eclair

1 strawberry, hulled
1 lime wedge
1/2 measure Frangelico hazelnut liqueur
1/2 measure wild strawberry liqueur
ice cubes

Muddle the strawberry and the lime wedge in a cocktail shaker. Add the liqueurs and some ice cubes, then shake briefly and strain into a shot glass.

B-4-12

1/2 measure Amaretto di Saronno liqueur
1/2 measure Baileys Irish Cream
1/2 measure chilled Absolut Kurant vodka

Pour the Amaretto di Saronno into a shot glass. Using the back of a bar spoon, slowly float the Baileys over the Amaretto. Pour the Absolut Kurant over the Baileys in the same way.

B-4-12

Absinthe Minded

Sake-tini

ice cubes
2½ measures sake
1 measure vodka
½ measure orange Curaçao
2 thin cucumber wheels, to decorate

Put the ice cubes into a mixing glass, add the sake, vodka, and Curaçao and stir well. Strain into a chilled cocktail glass and add two cucumber wheels, which are made by peeling the cucumber in strips lengthwise and then thinly slicing.

Absinthe Minded

ice cubes
1 measure absinthe
1 dash fresh lemon juice
1 dash Chambord raspberry liqueur

Put some ice cubes into a cocktail shaker with all the ingredients and shake briefly. Strain into a chilled shot glass.

Money Shot

1 measure well-chilled Jagermeister
1 measure well-chilled Rumple Minze (peppermint liqueur)

Pour the Jagermeister into a shot glass. Using the back of a bar spoon, slowly float the Rumple Minze over the Jagermeister.

QF

1/2 measure Kahlúa
dash Midori melon liqueur
1/2 measure Baileys Irish Cream

Pour the Kahlúa into a shot glass. Using the back of a bar spoon, slowly float the Midori over the Kahlúa. Float the Baileys over the Midori in the same way.

QF

Batida

crushed ice
2 measures cachaça
$\frac{1}{2}$ measure sugar syrup
$\frac{1}{2}$ measure fresh lemon juice
3 measures fruit juice (strawberry, pineapple, or mango)

Fill a highball glass with crushed ice. Pour the cachaça, sugar syrup, and fruit juices into the glass and stir to mix thoroughly.

Cowgirl

1 measure chilled peach schnapps
½ measure Baileys Irish Cream
peach wedge, to decorate

Pour the chilled schnapps into a shot glass. Using the back of a bar spoon, slowly layer the Baileys over the schnapps. Place a peach wedge on the rim of the glass, to be eaten after the shot has been drunk.

Pansy

ice cubes
1/2 measure Pernod
several dashes grenadine
few dashes Angostura bitters
lemon zest twist, to decorate

Put some ice cubes into a cocktail shaker and pour the Pernod, grenadine, and bitters over them. Shake well. Pour into a chilled cocktail glass and decorate with a lemon zest twist.

Cucumber Sake-tini

ice cubes
2 1/2 measures cucumber-infused sake
1 1/2 measures gin
1/2 measure orange Curaçao
peeled cucumber slices, to decorate

Put some ice cubes in a mixing glass with all the other ingredients and stir until thoroughly chilled. Strain into a chilled Martini glass. Decorate with peeled cucumber slices.

Cucumber Sake-tini

Grappa Strega

ice cubes
1 measure grappa (Italian grape brandy)
1 measure Strega herbal liqueur
1 tablespoon lemon juice
1 tablespoon orange juice

Put some ice cubes into a mixing glass. Pour the grappa, Strega, and fruit juices over the ice and stir. Strain into a chilled Martini glass.

Grappa Manhattan

ice cubes
2 measures grappa (Italian grape brandy)
1 measure Martini Rosso
1/2 measure Maraschino liqueur
2 dashes Angostura bitters
olives, to decorate

Put some ice cubes into a mixing glass. Pour the grappa, Martini, Maraschino liqueur, and bitters over the ice and stir. Strain into a chilled Martini glass and decorate with olives.

Grappa Manhattan

Original Pisco Sour

Kiwi Caipiroska

1/2 kiwifruit, peeled
1/2 lime, cut into wedges
2 teaspoons sugar syrup
crushed ice
2 measures vodka
2 teaspoons kiwifruit schnapps
kiwifruit slice, to decorate

Muddle the kiwifruit, lime, and sugar syrup in an old-fashioned glass. Fill the glass with crushed ice, then add the vodka and stir. Add more ice, then drizzle the schnapps over the surface and decorate with a kiwifruit slice.

Original Pisco Sour

ice cubes
2 measures Pisco (South American grape brandy)
1 measure lemon juice
2 teaspoons superfine sugar
1 egg white
3 dashes Angostura bitters
lemon wedges, to decorate (optional)

Put some ice cubes into a cocktail shaker with the Pisco, lemon juice, sugar, and egg white and shake well. Strain into an old-fashioned glass. Add the bitters to the drink's frothy head and decorate with lemon wedges, if you wish.

Papa G

ice cubes
1 measure Amaretto di Saronno liqueur
1 dash lemon juice
1 dash sugar syrup
1 drop Angostura bitters

Put some ice cubes into a cocktail shaker with all the ingredients and shake briefly. Strain into a shot glass.

Happiness is.....finding two olives in your martini when you're hungry. JOHNNY CARSON

Banshee

ice cubes
1 measure white crème de cacao
1 measure crème de banane
1 measure light cream

Put some ice cubes into a cocktail shaker. Pour the crème de cacao, crème de banane, and cream over the ice. Shake vigorously. Strain and serve straight up.

PCP

ice cubes
¾ measure Xante pear liqueur
1 dash strawberry liqueur
1 dash pear liqueur
1 dash lemon juice
1 dash vanilla syrup

Put some ice cubes into a cocktail shaker with all the other ingredients and shake briefly. Strain into a chilled shot glass.

PCP

Velvet Hammer

ice cubes
1 measure Cointreau
1 measure Tia Maria
1 measure cream

Fill a cocktail shaker three-quarters full with ice cubes. Add all the other ingredients and shake well. Strain into a chilled cocktail glass.

Caipirinha

1 lime, quartered
2 teaspoons cane sugar
crushed ice
2 measures cachaça

Muddle the lime quarters and sugar in an old-fashioned glass. Fill it with crushed ice and pour the cachaça over it. Stir and add more ice if needed.

Caipirinha

Atacama Pisco Sour

crushed ice
1½ measures Pisco (South American grape brandy)
½ measure blended Scotch whiskey
1 measure lemon juice
1 measure sugar syrup
grated lemon zest, to decorate

Put a small scoop of crushed ice with the Pisco, whiskey, lemon juice, and sugar syrup into a blender and blend until smooth. Pour into a Margarita glass and decorate with grated lemon zest.

383

1 teaspoon Frangelico hazelnut liqueur
1 measure chilled Stolichnaya Razberi vodka
orange wedge dusted with sugar, to decorate

Put the Frangelico liqueur into a shot glass, then add the vodka. Decorate with the sugared orange wedge. Drink the shot in one gulp, then eat the orange wedge.

Strawberry and Hazelnut Lassi

crushed ice
3 strawberries, hulled
⅓ banana
1 measure Frangelico hazelnut liqueur
1 measure Baileys Irish Cream
2 measures natural yogurt
3 mint leaves, plus 1 sprig to decorate

Put a scoop of crushed ice into a blender with all the other ingredients and blend until smooth. Pour into a tall sling glass and decorate with a mint sprig.

Fireball

½ measure ice-cold kümmel
½ measure Goldschlager
½ measure absinthe

Pour the kümmel into a shot glass. Using the back of a bar spoon, slowly float the Goldschlager over the kümmel. Pour the absinthe over the Goldschlager in the same way.

I drink to make other people interesting. GEORGE JEAN NATHAN

Classic Pimm's

On the Lawn

On the Lawn

ice cubes
1 measure Pimm's No 1
1 measure gin
2 measures lemonade
2 measures dry ginger ale
cucumber strips, to decorate
blueberries, to decorate
orange slices, to decorate

Fill a highball glass with ice cubes, then add the Pimm's, gin, lemonade, and dry ginger ale. Decorate with cucumber strips, blueberries, and orange slices.

Classic Pimm's

2 measures Pimm's No 1
6–8 ice cubes
orange, lemon and cucumber slices
4 measures lemonade
mint or borage sprigs, to decorate

Pour the Pimm's into a highball glass, add the ice cubes and the fruit and cucumber slices, then pour in the lemonade. Decorate with mint or borage sprigs.

Moth & Moose

½ measure Passoa passion fruit liqueur
½ measure Grey Goose l'Orange vodka

Pour the Passoa into a shot glass. Using the back of a bar spoon, slowly float the vodka over the Passoa.

Grasshopper

1 measure crème de cacao
1 measure crème de menthe
⅓ measure light cream
mint sprig, to decorate

Pour the crème de cacao into a cocktail glass. Using the back of a bar spoon, float the crème de menthe over the crème de cacao. Then float the cream over the crème de menthe in the same way. Serve decorated with a mint sprig.

Grasshopper

Batida Maracuja

ice cubes, plus crushed ice, to serve
2 measures cachaça
pulp of 2 passion fruit
1 measure sugar syrup
1 measure lemon juice
lemon slices, to decorate

Put some ice cubes into a cocktail shaker with the cachaça, passion fruit
pulp, sugar syrup, and lemon juice and shake. Strain into a highball glass
filled with crushed ice. Decorate with lemon slices.

'The worst thing about some
men is that when they are not
drunk they are sober.'

WILLIAM BUTLER YEATS

Brain Hemorrhage

1 measure peach schnapps
1 dash Baileys Irish Cream
3 drops grenadine

Pour the schnapps into a chilled shot glass. Using the back of a bar spoon, slowly float the Baileys over the schnapps. Very gently, drop the grenadine on top of the Baileys – it will gradually ease through this top layer.

Meet me down in the bar!
We'll drink breakfast together.

T. FROTHINGILL BELLOWS (W. C. FIELDS) –

THE BIG BROADCAST OF 1938 (1937)

Bubble Gum

ice cubes
½ measure Pisang Ambon liqueur
½ measure Malibu
1 dash fraise liqueur
1 dash pineapple juice

Put some ice cubes into a cocktail shaker with all the ingredients and shake briefly. Strain into a shot glass.

Dost thou think, because thou art virtuous, there shall be no more cakes and ale?

WILLIAM SHAKESPEARE, TWELFTH NIGHT

Flaming Lamborghini

1 measure Kahlúa
1 measure Sambuca
1 measure Baileys Irish Cream
1 measure blue Curaçao

Pour the Kahlúa into a warmed cocktail glass. Gently pour half the Sambuca over the back of a spoon into the cocktail glass, so that it floats on top. Pour the Baileys and the blue Curaçao into 2 shot glasses. Next, pour the remaining Sambuca into a warmed wine glass and carefully set it alight. Pour it into the cocktail glass with care. Pour the Baileys and Curaçao into the lighted cocktail glass at the same time. Serve with a straw.

It provokes the desire but it takes away the performance.

SHAKESPEARE, MACBETH

502

B-52

¹/₂ measure Kahlúa
¹/₂ measure Baileys Irish Cream
¹/₂ measure Grand Marnier

Pour the Kahlúa into a shot glass. Using the back of a bar spoon, slowly float the Baileys over the Kahlúa. Float the Grand Marnier over the Baileys in the same way.

One can drink too much, but
one never drinks enough.

GOTTHOLD EPHRAIM LESSING

VIRGIN COCKTAILS

Bitter Sweet

crushed ice
²/3 cup sparkling mineral water
2 dashes Angostura bitters
6–8 mint leaves
lemon or lime slices, to decorate

Put the crushed ice into a cocktail shaker, pour 2 tablespoons of the mineral water and the bitters over itand add the mint leaves. Shake until a frost forms. Pour into a chilled glass, top up with the remaining mineral water, and decorate with lemon or lime slices.

Virgin Colada

crushed ice
1 measure coconut cream
2 measures pineapple juice
pineapple wedge, to decorate

Put some crushed ice into a blender or food processor with the coconut cream and pineapple juice and blend, or shake in a cocktail shaker. Pour into a tall glass and decorate with a pineapple wedge.

Virgin Colada

Frosty Lime

1 scoop lime sorbet
1 measure grapefruit juice
4 teaspoons mint syrup
mint strips, to decorate
lemon slices, to decorate

Put the sorbet, grapefruit juice, and syrup into a blender or food processor and blend at high speed for about 30 seconds. Strain into a Champagne glass and decorate with mint strips and lemon slices.

Cranberry Crush

crushed ice
1.8 litres (3 pints) cranberry juice
600ml (1 pint) orange juice
600ml (1 pint) dry ginger ale
orange and lemon wedges, to decorate

Half-fill a large punch bowl with crushed ice. Pour in the fruit juices and stir to mix. Top up with the dry ginger ale and decorate with orange and lemon wedges. Serves 15

Cranberry
Crush

Keep Sober

ice cubes
½ measure grenadine
½ measure lemon syrup
3 measures tonic water
soda water, to top up

Put some ice cubes into a tumbler with the grenadine, lemon syrup, and tonic water and stir together. Top up with soda water.

Cool Passion

2 cups orange and passion fruit juice
4 cups pineapple juice
6 cups lemonade
crushed ice
blackberries, to decorate
mint sprigs, to decorate

Pour the juices into a large jug. Stir well to mix. Just before serving, stir in the lemonade. Pour into glasses filled with crushed ice and decorate each with a blackberry and a mint sprig. Serves 20

Cool Passion

Peach, Pear, and Raspberry Crush

crushed ice
1 ripe peach, skinned, pitted, and chopped
1 ripe pear, peeled, cored, and chopped
1 cup raspberries
7 measures peach juice
pear slices, to decorate

Put some crushed ice into a blender or food processor with the peach, pear, raspberries, and peach juice and blend until smooth. Serve in cocktail glasses and decorate with pear slices. Serves 2–3

Warbine Cooler

2 dashes Angostura bitters
1 dash lime juice
ginger beer, to top up
lime slices, to decorate

Stir the bitters and lime juice together in a large wine glass. Top up with ginger beer and decorate with lime slices. Serve with a straw.

Limeade

6 limes
1/44 cup superfine sugar
3 cups boiling water
pinch of salt
ice cubes
lime wedges, to decorate
mint leaves, to decorate

Halve the limes, then squeeze the juice into a large jug. Put the squeezed
lime halves into a heatproof jug with the sugar and boiling water and leave
to infuse for 15 minutes. Add the salt, stir the infusion well, then strain it
into the jug with the lime juice. Add 6 ice cubes, cover and chill for 2 hours
or until chilled. To serve, put 3–4 ice cubes in each glass and pour the
limeade over them. Add a lime wedge and a mint leaf to decorate.
Serves 8

Midsummer Punch

$^1/_2$ cup sugar
$1^1/_4$ cups water
$1^1/_4$ cups orange juice
$1^1/_4$ cups pineapple juice
$2^1/_2$ cups cold weak tea, strained
orange, lemon, apple, and pineapple slices
crushed ice
$1^1/_4$ cups dry ginger ale
mint sprigs, to decorate

Put the sugar and water into a saucepan and stir over a low heat until the sugar has dissolved. Leave to cool, then pour into a large jug or bowl. Stir in the fruit juices and cold tea, then add the fruit slices and some crushed ice. To serve, pour into tall glasses and top up with the dry ginger ale. Decorate with mint sprigs. Serves 8–10

Honeymoon

crushed ice
1 measure clear honey or maple syrup
4 teaspoons lime juice
1 measure orange juice
1 measure apple juice
maraschino cherry, to decorate

Put some crushed ice into a cocktail shaker and add the honey or maple syrup and the fruit juices. Shake well, then strain into a chilled cocktail glass. Decorate with a maraschino cherry impaled on a toothpick.

Honeymoon

Grapefruit Cooler

$^1/_2$ cup sugar
4 measures water
handful of mint sprigs, plus extra to decorate
juice of 4 large lemons
2 cups grapefruit juice
crushed ice
soda water, to top up

Put the sugar and water into a heavy-based saucepan and stir over a low heat until the sugar has dissolved. Leave to cool. Crush the mint leaves and stir into the syrup. Cover and leave to stand for about 12 hours, then strain into a jug. Add the fruit juices to the strained syrup and stir well. Fill 6 old-fashioned glasses or tumblers with crushed ice and pour the cooler into the glasses. Top up with soda water and decorate with mint sprigs. Serves 6

Tropical Treat

4 cups plain yogurt
1 large ripe pineapple, peeled and roughly chopped
$1^1/_4$ cups sparkling mineral water
ice cubes
sugar syrup, to taste
mint sprigs, to decorate

Put the yogurt, pineapple, and mineral water into a food processor and blend until smooth, in batches if necessary. Put the ice cubes into a tall pitcher, then pour in the drink through a very fine strainer. Stir, then add sugar syrup to taste and stir again. Pour into tall glasses and decorate with mint sprigs. Serves 4

Grapefruit Cooler

Alcohol-free Sangria

4 cups orange juice
sugar syrup, to taste
8 cups red grape juice
juice of 6 lemons
juice of 6 limes
20–30 ice cubes
orange, lemon, and lime slices, to decorate

Pour the orange juice and sugar syrup, to taste, into a punch bowl and stir. Add the fruit juices and stir well to mix. Add the ice cubes, then float the fruit slices on top. Serves 20

Tenderberry

crushed ice
6–8 strawberries, hulled
1 measure grenadine
1 measure heavy cream
1 measure dry ginger ale
ground ginger
strawberry, to decorate

Put some crushed ice into a blender or food processor with the strawberries, grenadine, and cream and blend for 30 seconds. Pour into a glass. Add the dry ginger ale and stir. Sprinkle a little ground ginger on top and decorate with a strawberry.

Tenderberry

Anita

3 ice cubes
1 measure orange juice
1 measure lemon juice
3 dashes Angostura bitters
soda water, to top up
lemon and orange slices, to decorate

Put the ice cubes into a cocktail shaker. Pour in the fruit juices and bitters and shake well. Strain into a tumbler and top up with soda water. Decorate with lemon and orange slices.

Pink Tonic

4–6 ice cubes
2–3 dashes Angostura bitters
8 measures tonic water
lime wedge, to decorate

Put the ice cubes into a tumbler. Shake the bitters over the ice, add the tonic water and stir well. Decorate with a lime wedge.

Pink Tonic

River Cruise

3 cups cantaloupe melon pulp
grated zest and juice of 2 lemons
2 tablespoons sugar
2½ cups chilled soda water

Remove and discard any melon
seeds. Put the pulp into a blender
or food processor and blend until
smooth. Scrape the purée into a
large jug. Put the lemon zest and
juice into a small saucepan with the sugar and stir over a low heat until the
sugar has dissolved. Strain the lemon mixture into the melon purée, mix
well, and chill. Stir in the chilled soda water just before serving. Serves 4–6

Prohibition Punch

4 measures sugar syrup
12 measures lemon juice
4 cups apple juice
ice cubes
2½ cups dry ginger ale
orange slices, to decorate

Put the sugar syrup and fruit juices
into a large chilled jug and stir.
Add the ice cubes and pour in the
dry ginger ale. Decorate with
orange slices. Serves 25–30

Carrot Cream

5 ice cubes
2 measures carrot juice
3 measures light cream
1 egg yolk
1 measure orange juice
orange slices, to decorate

Put the ice cubes into a tall glass.
Put the carrot juice, cream, egg
yolk and orange juice into a
cocktail shaker and shake well. Pour the carrot drink over the ice.
Decorate with orange slices and serve immediately.

Grenadine Soda

1/2 scoop orange sorbet
1/2 scoop raspberry sorbet
1 1/2 tablespoons grenadine
juice of 1/2 lime
1 scoop vanilla ice cream
4 measures soda water
finely chopped orange slice, to
    decorate
raspberries, to decorate

Put the sorbets, grenadine and lime juice into a blender or food processor
and blend until slushy. Pour into a glass and put the vanilla ice cream on
top. Top up with soda water. Stir gently and decorate with the finely

Jersey Lily

ice cubes
5 measures sparkling apple juice
2 dashes Angostura bitters
¼ teaspoon superfine sugar
maraschino cherry, to decorate

Put some ice cubes into a cocktail shaker with the apple juice, bitters, and sugar. Shake well, then strain into a wine glass. Decorate with a maraschino cherry.

What is a cocktail dress? Something to spill cocktails on.

DR. LAWRENCE BRADFORD (WILLIAM POWELL) & PAULA
BRADFORD (JEAN ARTHUR) – THE EX-MRS. BRADFORD (1936)

San Francisco

3 ice cubes
1 measure orange juice
1 measure lemon juice
1 measure pineapple juice
1 measure grapefruit juice
2 dashes grenadine
1 egg white
soda water, to top up
lemon and lime slices, to decorate
maraschino cherry, to decorate
orange zest spiral, to decorate

Put the ice cubes into a cocktail shaker and pour in the fruit juices, grenadine, and egg white. Shake well, then strain into a large goblet. Top up with soda water and decorate with lemon and lime slices, a maraschino cherry impaled on a toothpick, and an orange zest spiral. Serve with straws.

It takes a special talent to be a drunk. It takes endurance. Endurance is more important than truth.

HENRY – BARFLY (1987)

Florentine Coffee

hot espresso coffee
1 drop almond essence
1 sugar cube (optional)

Pour the coffee into a warmed cup or
heatproof glass. Add the almond
essence and sugar, if using, and stir.

Romanov Fizz

1 ice cube
4–5 ripe strawberries, hulled
2 measures orange juice
2 measures soda water

Put the strawberries and orange juice
into a blender or food processor and
blend until smooth. Put the ice cube
into a sour or wine glass and add the
strawberry liquid. Pour the soda water into the blender or food processor,
blend briefly and use to top up the glass. Stir briskly and serve.

Clayton's Pussyfoot

3 ice cubes, cracked
½ measure lemon syrup
½ measure orange juice
1 measure cola

Put all the ingredients into a cocktail shaker and shake well. Strain into a cocktail glass.

Spiced Ginger Punch

2 oranges
cloves, to taste
½ inch piece of fresh ginger root, peeled and grated
2 quarts dry ginger ale
cinnamon stick

Stud the oranges with the cloves, then bake them in a preheated oven at 350°F for about 25 minutes, until they are a rich, golden color. Cut the oranges into slices using a sharp knife, then put them into a saucepan with the grated ginger, dry ginger ale, and the cinnamon stick. Bring steadily just to the boiling point, but do not boil. Remove the cinnamon stick, then pour the punch into heatproof glasses and serve. Serves 12

Nursery Fizz

crushed ice
3 measures orange juice
3 measures dry ginger ale
maraschino cherry, to decorate
orange slice, to decorate

Fill a large wine glass with crushed ice and pour in the orange juice and ginger ale. Decorate with a cherry and an orange slice impaled on a toothpick.

Coco-oco

crushed ice
4 teaspoons creamed coconut or coconut syrup
2 teaspoons lemon juice
1 teaspoon Maraschino syrup
3½ measures whole milk
4 dashes Angostura bitters
pineapple leaf and wedge, to decorate
maraschino cherry, to decorate

Put the crushed ice into a blender or food processor and add the creamed coconut or coconut syrup, lemon juice, Maraschino syrup, milk and bitters. Blend for a few seconds. Pour into a tall glass and decorate with a pineapple leaf and wedge and a maraschino cherry.

Coco-oco

BAR
BASICS

Equipment

Some pieces of equipment, such as shakers and decent glasses, are vital for any cocktail party, while others, like ice buckets, can be obtained later if needed. Below is a wish-list for anyone who wants to make cocktails regularly.

Shakers

The most obvious piece of equipment is a cocktail shaker. There are two basic types, European and Boston. The basic difference between the two is that the European shaker has an integral strainer, while the Boston shaker does not. One half of the Boston shaker may be made of glass and have measurements etched into it. When mixing different cocktails, it is vital that the shaker and other equipment be cleaned thoroughly and dried between cocktails. Imagine what a trace of coconut milk from a Piña Colada would do to the taste of a Vodka Martini…

Strainers

If you are using a Boston shaker, you will need something to strain the cocktails through. Although a small sieve would work, a proper cocktail strainer looks far more stylish. Some drinks require double-straining for extra smoothness.

Measures

Getting the balance of flavors right is important for all cocktails, so the different ingredients need to be measured accurately. A set of measures makes this much easier. It is also far easier to make layered drinks by pouring the liqueurs from a measure than when trying to hold a heavy bottle steady.

Utensils

As so many drinks contain, or are decorated with, fruit, a good, sharp knife and a chopping board are essential. You will also need spoons for stirring and muddling drinks, and for when floating one liqueur over another in layered drinks. A long-handled bar spoon is perfect for this. Try to get one with a spiral handle as this will make creating citrus zest spirals much easier. Although these can be made with a small, sharp knife, a fruit zester makes this job easier. Tongs or a small scoop for ice are useful and an ice bucket may be helpful. A machine for crushing ice might be a boon if you are making cocktails regularly, but otherwise a clean tea towel, a plastic bag, and a wooden rolling pin will suffice. A good corkscrew is a must and while a fork can be used to beat egg whites, using a small whisk is quicker.

Equipment for decorating

Many drinks are decorated with fruit impaled on toothpicks and these are available in wood, plastic, or glass. Exotic drinks may be prettified with a paper umbrella and several long drinks are served with straws or swizzle sticks.

Glasses

In order to serve cocktails, it is important to have good-quality glasses that are appropriate to the drinks. Cheap glasses will spoil both the look and the taste of your drinks, so making your efforts a waste of time.

Nowadays, cocktails are divided into several groups, loosely characterized by the type of glass in which they are served.

Classic cocktails, such as Manhattans, are, naturally enough, served in long-stemmed cocktail glasses. They are mostly either stirred or shaken with ice—in the case of the Martini, whether to shake or stir has been a subject of debate for years—and then strained into a glass. Margaritas are served in their own glasses, while Daiquiris can be served in either type.

Long drinks, such as Gin Fizz and Cuba Libre, are generally served in highball glasses, although you could also buy

sling, hurricane, and Collins glasses. Long drinks are usually a combination of spirits and a mixer such as fruit juice or soda water. Most are served over ice. They are often decorated with fruit.

Short drinks, such as Mai Tai, Negroni, and Screwdriver, usually consist of a mixture of two liquor or one liquor and a small amount of mixer. They are served in heavy-bottomed, old-fashioned glasses —known as rocks or lowball glasses— although some can be served in cocktail glasses. Like long drinks, these are meant for sipping slowly, and many are served with copious amounts of crushed ice. Sour glasses can probably wait until later.

Champagne cocktails, such as Bellini and Black Velvet, and those made with other sparkling wines are served in tall Champagne flutes or wide Champagne saucers. Punches are served from a large bowl into individual glasses.

Shots are extra-short drinks, designed to be drunk in one go. Some, like the Tequila Slammer, consist of a single spirit, although others, like Slippery Nipple, are layered.

Ingredients

It would be impossible to stock the ingredients necessary for every conceivable cocktail, so it is best to think about what you are planning to do. If you are going to serve a few select cocktails, you can limit what you buy, but if you are planning to do it in style, you will need a larger selection. The best idea in this case is to buy the ingredients for several of the most popular cocktails and gradually add to them. No one will be surprised if your cocktail bar is not stocked like Dean Martin's. However, if you know one of your guests has a favorite cocktail, make sure you have the ingredients needed. You can also suit

suit the drinks to the occasion: people will probably want different drinks before an alfresco summer lunch than they do at an evening cocktail party in winter.

Liquid ingredients

Start off with those commonly used in cocktails: gin, whiskey, rum, vodka, brandy, and tequila, as well as sparkling wines and Champagne. Added to this, you will want to have to hand all the basic mixers, such as soda water, tonic water, cola, lemonade, and fruit juices, as well as commonly used flavorings, syrups and other ingredients. Dry and sweet vermouth occur in quite a few gin- and vodka-based cocktails, so are good staples.

For shots, it may be best to concentrate on the ingredients for a few popular ones—there is little point in buying expensive ingredients that will just sit on a shelf untouched.

Other ingredients

Make sure you have other ingredients that you might need, such as cream, cocoa, coconut milk, salt, pepper, Tabasco sauce, Worcestershire sauce and eggs.

Ice

Ice is an integral part of making all but a few cocktails, so you need plenty of this. If you have an ice-maker in your refrigerator, make sure you empty it regularly over the preceding few days so you have a good stock of ice. Otherwise, buy a couple of bags of ice cubes the day before and put them in the freezer. When drinks are served with ice, always put as much ice in as the recipe calls for. Although you might think that more ice would dilute the drink, in fact it has the opposite effect. With more ice in, the drink stays chilled for longer so the ice does not melt.

Flavorings and decorations

Lemons, limes, and oranges are musts, as are green olives and maraschino cherries. Other fruit that it is good to have to hand are apples, pineapple, and bananas. Mint appears as a decoration or flavoring in so many cocktails that it is a good idea to have a packet in the refrigerator.

Try to use the fruits mentioned for decorations, although these can be substituted when a particular fruit is not in season. However, if a particular fruit is an integral part of the drink, it is best not to experiment.

Techniques

Although watching an experienced barman juggling a cocktail shaker round the bar can be enjoyable, it is not actually necessary to do this in order to mix a cocktail well, although that does not mean you cannot have fun practicing.

Chilling
Always make sure that the glasses and cocktail shaker are cold. Glasses can be put into the freezer for an hour or so before use. If washing up the shaker between mixing drinks, run it under cold water before drying it off. Serve drinks as soon as possible after they are finished, in order to prevent them warming up.

Mixing drinks
There are two methods of doing this, shaking and stirring. The first incorporates the various liquids used in a drink thoroughly and chills them. It is important to shake the ingredients really thoroughly to mix them and cool them down. When flavorings such as berries are used, shaking extracts their flavors. Drinks are stirred in the glass when the ingredients combine easily. Always stir gently, to avoid incorporating air or breaking the ice cubes.

Muddling
Muddling is used in such drinks as Mint Julep. It means to crush the ingredients in the bottom of a glass to extract their flavor before the alcohol is added.

Layering
This technique, used in shots, and such drinks as Irish Coffee takes time to master. Pour the first ingredient into the glass and then add the second by pouring it gently over the back of a bar spoon held just above the first ingredient. It is important to add the liqueurs in the order specified in the recipe, that is, heaviest liqueur first, otherwise a heavier liquid will simply sink through a lighter one below and spoil the effect.

Decorating with fruit
Fruit wedges are a popular addition to many cocktails and are simple to make. They can be perched on the side of the glass, or dropped or squeezed in. Citrus wedges can be done in advance if you wish, but apples, pineapple, and bananas are best done at the last moment. Small clusters of berries, such as redcurrants, can be draped over the rim of a glass, while maraschino cherries, berries such as

raspberries and blackberries, and wedges of larger fruit can be speared on toothpicks, and balanced on the rim or dropped into a short glass.

Citrus zest can be formed into twists or spirals to dangle over the edge of a glass. Spirals are cut with a parer or small sharp knife, while twists are wider and so better cut with a vegetable peeler. For a twist, wrap the cut length round the handle of a bar spoon, or a straw or swizzle stick. Hold it for a few minutes and as its essential oils evaporate, it will dry into a spiral. Try squeezing the juice from a citrus twist onto the top of the drink for extra zing. To flame a citrus twist, hold a piece of zest with no pith attached skin-side down about 4 inches above the drink in one hand with a long lighted match in the other. Pinch the zest firmly so that the oils spray into the flame and ignite onto the drink.

Frosting
This technique, best known in the Margarita, is worth mastering. The rim of the glass is dipped into a shallow dish of beaten egg white, water, or citrus juice and then rolled in, for example salt, sugar, or cocoa.

PHOTOGRAPHY
© Octopus Publishing Group Limited

Lemon Martini
Leo
Leprechaun Dancer
Lime Fizz
Limeade
Limon Mojito
Lobsters on South Beach
Loving Cup
Luigi
Lush Crush
Lynchburg Lemonade

Machete
Mafia Martini
Mai Tai
Maiden's Blush
Maiden's Prayer
Man in the Moon
Mango Bellini
Manhattan
Maracuja
Margarita
Marguerite
Martini Royale
Mbolero
Melbourne
Melon Ball
Metropolitan
Mexican Bulldog
Mexican Mule
Mexicana
Mexicola
Midsummer Punch
Mike Collins
Mint Julep I
Mint Julep II
Mississippi Mule
Mississippi Punch
Mockingbird
Mojito
Money Shot
Monkey Gland
Monoloco Zombie
Monta Rosa
Monte Carlo Sling

Moon River
Morning
Moscow Mule
Moth & Moose
Mudslide
Murray Hearn
My Tie Collection

Negroni
Nerida
New Day
New Orleans Dandy
New Orleans Dry Martini
New Yorker
Nice Pear
Night of Passion
North Pole
Nursery Fizz

October Revolution
On the Lawn
One of Those
Opal Martini
Opera
Orange Blossom
Original Pisco Sour
Oyster Shot

Paddy's Night
Pale Original
Pancho Villa
Pansy
Papa Doble, The
Papa G
Paradise
Parisian Spring Punch
Parisien
Park Lane Special
Parrot's Head Punch
Passion for Fashion
Passion Fruit Margarita
PCP
PDQ

Peach, Pear and Raspberry Crush
Penguin
Perfect Lady
Pernod Fizz
Pillow Talk
Piña Colada
Pineapple Mojito
Pink Angel
Pink Cadillac Convertible
Pink Camellia
Pink Clover Club
Pink Gin
Pink Mojito
Pink Tonic
Pink Treasure
Planter's Punch
Plasma
Playa Del Mar
Poet's Dream
Polish Martini
Port Antonio
Prohibition Punch
Pudding Cocktail, The
Purple Haze

QF

Raspberry Beret
Rattlesnake
Razzamopolitan
Red Cloud
Red Kiss
Red Lion
Red Rum
Rhett Butler
Rickey
Rising Sun
Ritz Fizz I
Ritz Fizz II
Ritz Old-fashioned
River Cruise
Riviera Fizz
Road Runner
Roamin' the Gloamin'

40° proof—so juice, water, herbs, and spices would have helped to disguise the harsh taste. Different regions developed their own particular recipes, such as juleps in the southern states of America and a variety of punches in the Caribbean (although the latter probably originated in India).

Although the word cocktail is now used as a blanket term for a wide variety of mixed drinks—Slings, Sours, Punches, Martinis, Daiquiris, and many more—it was originally confined to a small group of drinks. One early reference—from 1806—describes a cocktail as "a stimulating liquor composed of spirits of any kind, sugar, water, and bitters – it is vulgarly called a bitter sling…". They appear to have been regarded as a sort of morning pick-me-up, possibly even a hangover cure. *The Bon Vivant's Companion: or how to mix drinks* of 1862 described cocktails as a handful of drinks that included bitters among their ingredients. Among the recipes is one for a Martinez, which later became the Martini.

During the second half of the 19th century, cocktail-drinking really took off. Famous drinks that came into being during this period include the Manhattan (which was invented in the 1870s for Winston Churchill's mother, socialite Jenny Jerome), while the Singapore Sling was invented in around 1910–15 in the Raffles Hotel in Singapore.

By this time, the prohibition lobby was gaining ground in the United States and in 1920 the manufacture, sale, and consumption of alcoholic drinks were forbidden, which simply sent the trade underground and helped to fuel organized crime. In Europe, however, life for the rich was far more liberated and cocktails continued to be enjoyed, often as pre-lunch appetizers and at cocktail parties. After prohibition ended in 1933, Hollywood films gave cocktails a glamorous image, and after the war, cocktail-drinking was still a mark of sophistication. In the 1970s, vodka took over from gin as the most popular liquor base for cocktails, which gave rise to a vast array of new drinks. Then, in the 1980s, with the advent of "happy hour", things changed. The young no longer wanted to sip classic cocktails, but to knock back new inventions such as Brain Hemorrhage, Dirty Sanchez, and Zombie. However, the 1988 film *Cocktail* sparked both a craze for "flair bartending" and a return to the classics, which have, thankfully, never really gone away.